Gift Favors

small gifts for all occasions

S0-BBM-267

By Basha Kooler

About the Author

Donna, Thea, and Basha

Drawing upon her background in advertising, art direction and graphic design, Basha Kooler is an accomplished craft designer, writer, and photo stylist for Kooler Design Studio. Besides utilizing her talents for styling the beautiful photographs in all of the KDS books, Basha has also written craft and home décor books and has contributed projects and designs to a variety of other KDS titles. She loves faux finishing old furniture, creating art from recycled objects, painting, and knitting. In addition to her many creative interests, Basha loves hiking, playing golf, exploring art galleries and museums, and especially spending quality time with her 12 year old daughter, Thea.

Dedication

I'm proud to be part of three generations of Kooler women. My mom, Donna, founder of Kooler Design Studio, and my daughter, Thea, both inspire me every day with their infinite wisdom, style, and intelligence. I learn so much from them and am so blessed to have them in my life. I want to thank everyone at Kooler Design Studio. My co-workers on this special team support each other and fill in the blanks as needed to make the studio such a fun, creative, and welcoming place to spend my days. Special thanks to Dianne Woods, our amazing photographer and great friend. Dianne makes every project look spectacular!

Contents

About the Author 2

Introduction. 5

Materials 6

Cucumber Kooler Toner 8

Espresso Yourself. 10

Bee My Honey. 12

Kung Hey Fat Choy 14

Incense Burner. 17

Herbes de Provence 20

Citrus Scented Bath Salts 22

Hidden Treasures. 24

Rose Water Glycerin Bath 26

Cranberry Lip Gloss. 28

Votives for All Occasions 30

Candlelight & Rosebuds 32

Seaside Bath Fizzies 34

Think Outside the Box. 36

Mardi Gras Cajun Spices 40

Swing Into Spring 42

Purses With Pizzazz 47

Terra Cotta Magnets 50

Haute Couture. 52

Princess Tea Party 54

Resources 57

Project Labels, Tags, and Patterns. . . 58

Gift Favors

By Basha Kooler

Delight the senses, *pamper* your guests, and let them know how special they are by sending them home with any one of the small gift favor projects contained within these pages.

Like my first book of favors, this book is chock full of small gifts that will appeal to all of the *senses* in addition to being playful, *elegant*, *colorful*, and a little *self indulgent*—hence the name Gift Favors as opposed to party *favors.* Many of these little *treasures* can be appropriate gifts for many different holidays and special occasions. I have left many of them generic so that YOU can adapt and *personalize* them for your special event.

Just think how nice it will be for your guests to feel an *invigorating* coffee body scrub, soak in a bath of citrus bath salts, or *luxuriate* with honey *conditioner*. Smell the *aroma* of a rose *scented* glycerin *bath* and *fragrant*, refreshing cool cucumber toner. Taste and *breathe* in the combinations of herbs and *spices* in the Herbes de Provence and Cajun style seasonings— all wrapped and packaged in *sweet,* simple little containers.

These *20* favor ideas, plus a multitude of variations, created by myself and a few friends, will inspire you to *celebrate* and pamper your guests with sensual, *whimsical* and *lovely* gifts that they will take home, use, and enjoy. We have created simple recipes and *clean - looking designs* that will be a snap to make for 5 or 50 party goers. We have found that getting ready for a *party* is at least half the *fun*...so sit back, breath deeply...choose your first *project*, and let the festivities begin. Enjoy!

Basha

Materials

Gathering Materials

A quick trip to the craft store and supermarket or health food store will provide you with everything you'll need to create most of these lovely small gifts. But before you head out for the store, check your pantry for common ingredients, such as coffee, brown sugar, and olive oil, to name just a few. Chances are you may already have these on hand. Also check your stash of craft supplies for ribbons, embellishments, punches, etc. that may work perfectly for your favors. Online stores offer some of the harder to find supplies, such as Dead Sea bath salts and quantities of small tin containers. Refer to page 57 for quick, affordable, and reliable sources for these.

Making Tags and Labels

Tags and/or labels add the perfect finishing touch to your favors. If you have access to a computer and printer, tags and labels are quite simple to make. Using Microsoft Word software, start by creating the text using fancy type fonts and desired colors (Format – Font). Then use the "shading" feature (Format – Borders and Shading) to add a colored background. Copy as many tags/labels as you need to the page, then print out on white card stock or paper. The tags and labels we have created for these projects are mostly generic, but you can add names, dates, and special occasions to further personalize your favors. Samples of generic tags are available in the back of the book for you to color photocopy if printing your own is not an option. Invest in a few 1" or larger decorative punches, several pair of decorative edge scissors and a ⅛" diameter hole punch to finish off the tags. Attach using ribbon or wire and embellish with a few beads. That is all you will need to finish these simply elegant gift favors.

Left to right: Dead Sea bath salts, vegetable glycerin, honey, rosewood essential oil, vitamin E oil, sweet almond oil, dried rosebuds, olive oil, jojoba oil, baking soda, witch hazel, glass bottles, tea light candle, metal tin, plastic jar, flower embellishments, printed tags and labels, circle template, flower punch, ribbons, wire, ⅛" hole punch, decorative edge scissors, decorative papers.

Cucumber Kooler Toner

Dabs of cool cucumber toner will bring refreshing relief on a hot summer day. Made from simple ingredients and packaged in small corked bottles from the local craft store or kitchen shop, this pampering and chilling gift is sure to please overstressed moms at a baby shower or new sorority sisters at a welcome party. An instant relaxer with a divine scent, just a dab to the back of your neck will make your spine tingle. Be sure to refrigerate this concoction and it will last for weeks, otherwise it will develop into an interesting science project within a week! Keep a bottle handy for cooling yourself until party time, and your friends will think YOU are totally cool!

Materials (per favor)

6 ounce clear glass bottle with cork approx. 4½" high
24-gauge black fun wire, approx. 20"
8 green faceted beads
Needle nose pliers
Colored paper tag
⅛" paper punch

Cucumber Toner Recipe

¼ cup cucumber juice (1 large cucumber makes approx. 1 cup of juice)
¼ cup witch hazel
¼ cup distilled water
Fine sieve or cheesecloth

Chop up cucumber, peel and all, and liquefy in a blender or food processor. Strain juice through a fine sieve or cheesecloth to remove pulp. Discard pulp or save for your favorite gazpacho recipe!

Mix together cucumber juice, witch hazel, and distilled water.

Instructions

Pour prepared toner into clean bottle. Seal with cork. Wrap black wire twice around the neck of the bottle, leaving a short and long end. String 3 green beads onto the short end and 5 beads onto the long end. Using needle nose pliers, coil the wires, spacing out beads as desired. Color-photocopy the cucumber slice tags on page 59 (or make your own). Punch a hole at the center top and attach to the neck wire. Store in refrigerator.

KoOleR
KoOleR
KoOleR
CucumbeR KoOleR
CucumbeR KoOleR
CucumbeR KoOleR
CucumbeR KoOleR
CucumbeR KoOleR
CucumbeR KoOleR

Espresso Yourself

The irresistible aroma of America's favorite drink is captured in this chic tin filled with an invigorating coffee and brown sugar based body scrub. The gals will love being surprised with this gift at your next bachelorette or slumber party. Similar products with hefty price tags are available at bath boutiques and health food stores, but you can make this scrub inexpensively using ground coffee, brown sugar, sweet almond oil, and essential oils of orange and lemon. The combination of coffee and citrus is invigorating and some say the caffeine in coffee redistributes fat cells and decreases cellulite along with shrinking and tightening blood vessels. It will take a little extra rinsing to clean up your shower, but the benefits are well worth it!

A label on the bottom of the tin gives instructions for use and a clever name for your scrub such as Espresso Yourself—or how about Java Sugar Scrub, Sumatra Sugar Scrub, or the name of your own local grind!

Materials (for 8 favors)

Eight 4 ounce tins with clear lids (2½" square)
(see resources on page 57)
Coffee scrub filling (see recipe)
One 12" x 12" piece patterned paper
Glue or double-sided tape
4½ yards patterned ribbon
Eight 2" square white labels

Coffee Scrub Recipe (for 8 favors)

1 cup coarse ground coffee
1 cup sweet almond oil
2 cups golden brown sugar
12 drops essential oil of sweet orange
12 drops essential oil of lemon

Pour ground coffee into a large bowl, slowly drizzle on oils, and mix until evenly distributed. Add sugar, mixing well to create a beautiful dark brown, heavenly scented mixture.

Instructions

Fill tins with scrub mixture to approximately ¼" from top. Cut eight 9" x ⅞" strips of patterned paper. Wrap a strip around the base of each tin, securing the ends with glue or tape. Cut the ribbon into eight 20" pieces. Tie a ribbon and bow around each tin. Color-photocopy the labels on page 58 or make your own with the name of your scrub, the contents, and use instructions. Use glue or double-sided tape to adhere a label to the bottom of each tin, holding ribbon in place.

Bee My Honey

Here's a sweet treat that's great for an engagement party favor or Valentine's Day gift. The honey, olive oil, and lavender essential oil create a deep penetrating hair conditioner that will leave hair looking soft and silky. The ingredients in this sweet, smooth mixture are all natural and even edible. So, if you prefer, you can add some white wine vinegar to the ingredients, and you'll have a delicious salad dressing. Just change the label to "Be My Honey Salad Dressing!"

Materials (per favor)

1¾" x 4" square glass spice bottle with cork stopper
Honey conditioner (see recipe)
½ yard ⅜" orange embroidered ribbon
Yellow label
Silver bee pin (see resources)
Glue

Honey Conditioner Recipe (for 8 favors)

4 cups honey
2 cup olive oil
8 drops essential oil of lavender
2 teaspoon xanthan gum
Mix all ingredients thoroughly in a bowl. (The xanthan gum acts as a stabilizer and emulsifier and keeps the mixture from separating.)

Instructions

Pour conditioner into spice bottles and seal each with a tight fitting cork stopper. Color-photocopy the labels on page 60 (or create your own). Wrap the ribbon around the neck of the bottle and crisscross the ends over one square edge for the front of the jar. Glue the label to the jar, securing the ribbon ends in place as shown. Push the bee pin into the cork top. Hand out little cards with use information (below) or print it on another label and glue to the back of the bottle.

Card or Label

To use: Apply a small amount to damp hair. Massage into scalp and wrap hair in a warm towel or shower cap for 20 minutes to deep condition. Rinse out with warm water and style as usual.

Bee
My Honey
***
Deep Conditioner
For hair
Bee
My Honey
***
Deep Conditioner
For hair
Bee
My Honey
***
Deep Conditioner
For hair
Bee
My Honey
***
Deep Conditioner
For hair
Bee
My Honey
Bee
My Honey
***

Kung Hey Fat Choy

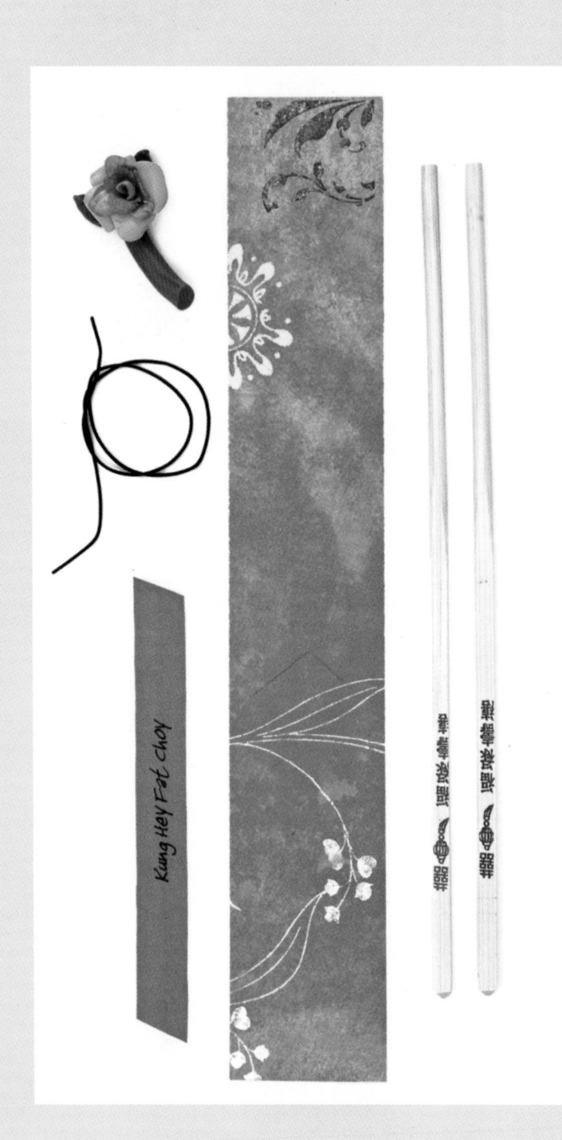

Having a Chinese New Year party, or Asian-themed birthday celebration? Send your guests home with chopsticks and a pretty rose rest, and they'll never use a fork for Chinese take out again. These colorful favors will brighten each table setting or make a striking centerpiece if placed in fan formation. The delightful roses are fun to make from polymer clay. When combined with import store chopsticks and classy packaging, this favor is sure to impress.

Materials (for 10 favors)

Four 2 ounce packages polymer clay: lime green, turquoise, red, bright orange (see resources)
Non stick craft sheet
Acrylic clay roller
Craft knife
Inexpensive chopsticks (from import store)
Two 12" x 12" heavyweight patterned paper
Colored paper label
Glue
Thin black cording

Instructions

Blending Clay Colors: Remove a portion of each color from the package and knead colors separately in your hands for a few minutes to soften and condition the clay. If the clay feels flexible and can be pulled easily without breaking immediately, it is ready to use. Shape each color into a rope then twist ropes together in the color combinations shown below to mix colors. Fold in half and twist again. Repeat this process until colors look well mixed.

Kung Hey Fat choy
Kung Hey Fat choy
Kung Hey Fat choy
Kung Hey Fat Choy
Kung Hey Fat Choy
Kung Hey Fat choy
Kung Hey Fat choy
Kung Hey Fat choy
Kung Hey Fat choy

Rose Chopstick Rest (per favor):

For stems and leaves mix 2 parts lime green + 1 part turquoise. Use the clay roller to roll a piece of green clay into a 3/16" thick slab and use a craft knife to cut out 2 small leaves measuring ¾" long [photo 1]. Form more clay into a roll measuring ¼" in diameter [photo 2]. Slice off 1¾" long sections and curve each section into a "C" shape. Attach two leaves near the top of each stem and fan out like "flippers on a seal" [photo 3]. These will serve as the supports for the chopstick rest.

For rose petals mix as follows:

- Center petals – 2 parts red hot red + 1 part glow-in-the-dark light orange (or substitute with ½ bright orange and ½ white if glow-in-the-dark clay is not available).
- Middle petals – Same as above, then add 1 part white; do not mix completely for a marbled look.
- Outer petals – Glow-in-the-dark light orange (or ½ bright orange and ½ white).

Form each of the three clay mixtures into a long roll measuring about ½" in diameter. Using the craft knife, cut 3/16" thick slices from the rolls. Press down on a slice with your finger to make a thin oval petal. Start with the darkest color for the center petals. Roll up one petal for the center [photo 4]. Using the same color, add two more petals around the center roll [photo 5]. Add four more petals of the lighter, marbled red around the center and then four of the orange petals to the outer edges [photo 6]. Curl up the tips of the petals. Carefully press a rose to the top of the uplifted stem as if it were the "head of the seal." Bake according to manufacturer's instructions and let cool.

Packaging: Cut heavyweight patterned paper into 2" wide pieces. Use a craft knife to cut 2 "V"s in each piece, spaced approximately 3" apart (see photo) for holding the chopsticks. Color-photocopy the "Kung Hey Fat Choy" labels on page 59 (or make your own). Cut out and glue diagonally across the paper between the "V" cuts. Insert chopsticks through the cuts as shown. Tie a 7" piece of thin black cording around the rose rest, chopsticks, and paper to hold all elements in place.

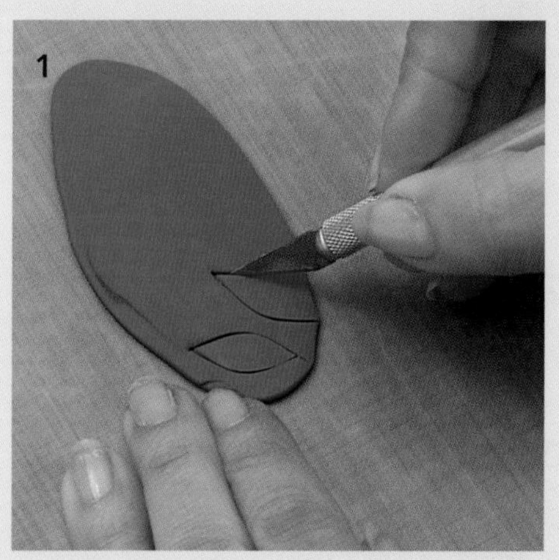

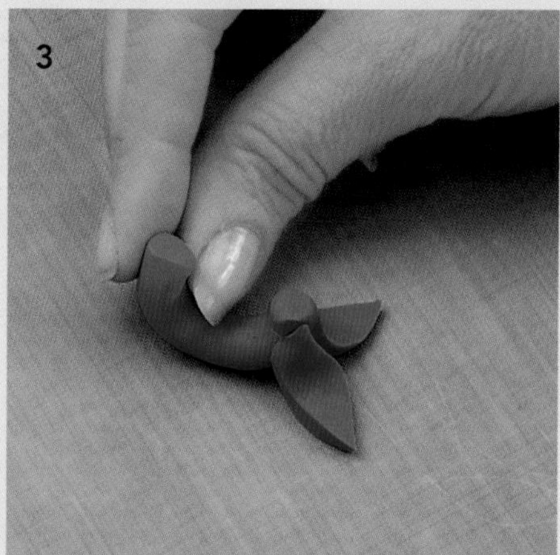

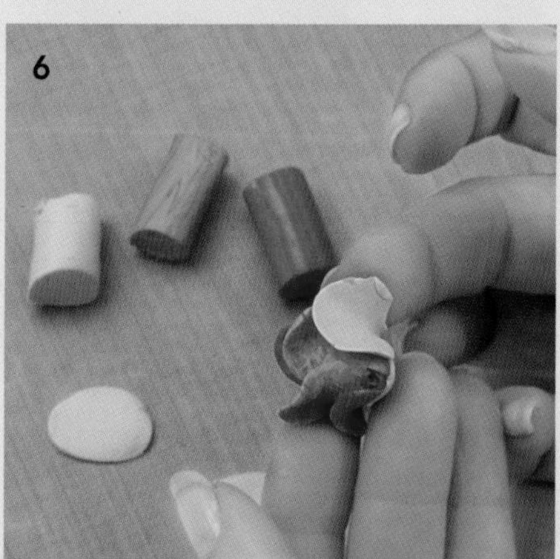

Incense Burner

Aromatherapy goes mainstream at a Far Eastern-themed party. A graceful flower holder with sweet smelling incense is the prize for each guest to take home. After a busy day, this unique favor will help them unwind as they breath in the relaxing aroma and de-stress. Can you think of a better gift to offer your guests than peace and tranquility?

Materials (for 12 favors)

Six 2 ounce packages polymer clay: lime green, white, glow-in-the-dark light green, hot pink, bright orange, yellow (see resources)
Craft knife
Awl or large tapestry needle
Leaf mold (see resources) or large waxy garden leaf with veining
14" clay roller
Non-stick craft sheet or other non-stick surface
White acrylic paint
Faux glazing medium
Incense sticks
Brown corrugated papers
Asian patterned and mulberry papers
Double -stick tape
Cellophane wrap
Thin metallic cording

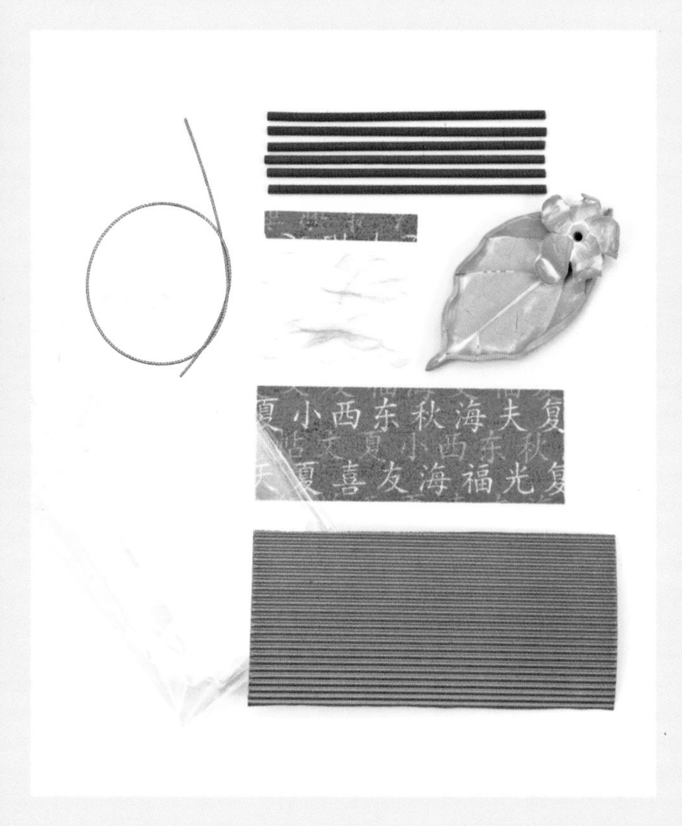

Instructions

Blending Clay Colors: Mix clay colors for the leaf and flower parts by conditioning the clay and blending. Remove a portion of each color from the package and knead colors separately in your hands for a few minutes. If the clay feels flexible and can be pulled easily without breaking immediately, it is ready to use. Shape each color into a rope then twist ropes together. Fold in half and twist again. Repeat this process until colors look well-mixed.

Leaf: Mix 1 part lime green + 2 parts white + 1 part glow-in-the-dark light green. Flatten 1" balls of green clay into 3⁄16" thick slabs using the clay roller [photos 1 and 2, page 19]. Press onto leaf mold to achieve veining then peel off [photos 3]. Using a craft knife, cut out a 2" x 3" leaf shape [photos 4]. Bend up the leaf edges for a natural scalloped look [photos 5]. Make a small ½" ball of green clay and press onto one end of the leaf to form the base for the flower.

Flower: Mix as follows: outer petal – 1 part hot pink + 1 part white; inner petal – 1 part bright orange + 1 part white; center – yellow. Make the petals by rolling the pink clay mixture into a long roll about ½" in diameter. Roll the orange clay mixture into a similar roll. Using the craft knife, cut 3⁄16" thick slices from the rolls. Place a small orange slice at one edge of a pink slice and

press down with your finger to make a thin oval petal [photos 6]. Arrange five petals on top of the green ball, overlapping slightly, and press down to attach [photos 7]. Curl up outside edges of petals. Add a tiny, yellow ball of clay to the center of the flower and make a ½" hole into the flower and ball for holding the incense stick [photos 8]. Angle the hole so the incense stick will lean slightly over the leaf area when burning and this will catch any ash that accumulates. Bake according to the manufacturer's instructions, using a non-stick craft sheet; let cool. Finish with a whitewash glaze made from 1 part white acrylic paint + 3 parts faux glazing medium. Wipe on and wipe off with a soft cloth, leaving paint in cracks and veins of leaf and flower. This will give a subtle eggshell finish.

Packaging: Cut a 2" x 5" piece of brown corrugated paper and a 4¼" x 1½" piece of Asian patterned paper. Glue the patterned paper to the center of the corrugated paper. Use a 1½" strip of mulberry paper to wrap a bundle of 6 incense sticks together, securing with double-sided tape, then wrap a 3/16" band of patterned paper over the mulberry paper (see photo, page 18). Attach the incense bundle to the paper base, using double-sided tape. Create a bag for the assembled favor using an 8" x 18" piece of cellophane. Insert the favor, gather the open end together, and tie closed, using a 9" piece of metallic cording.

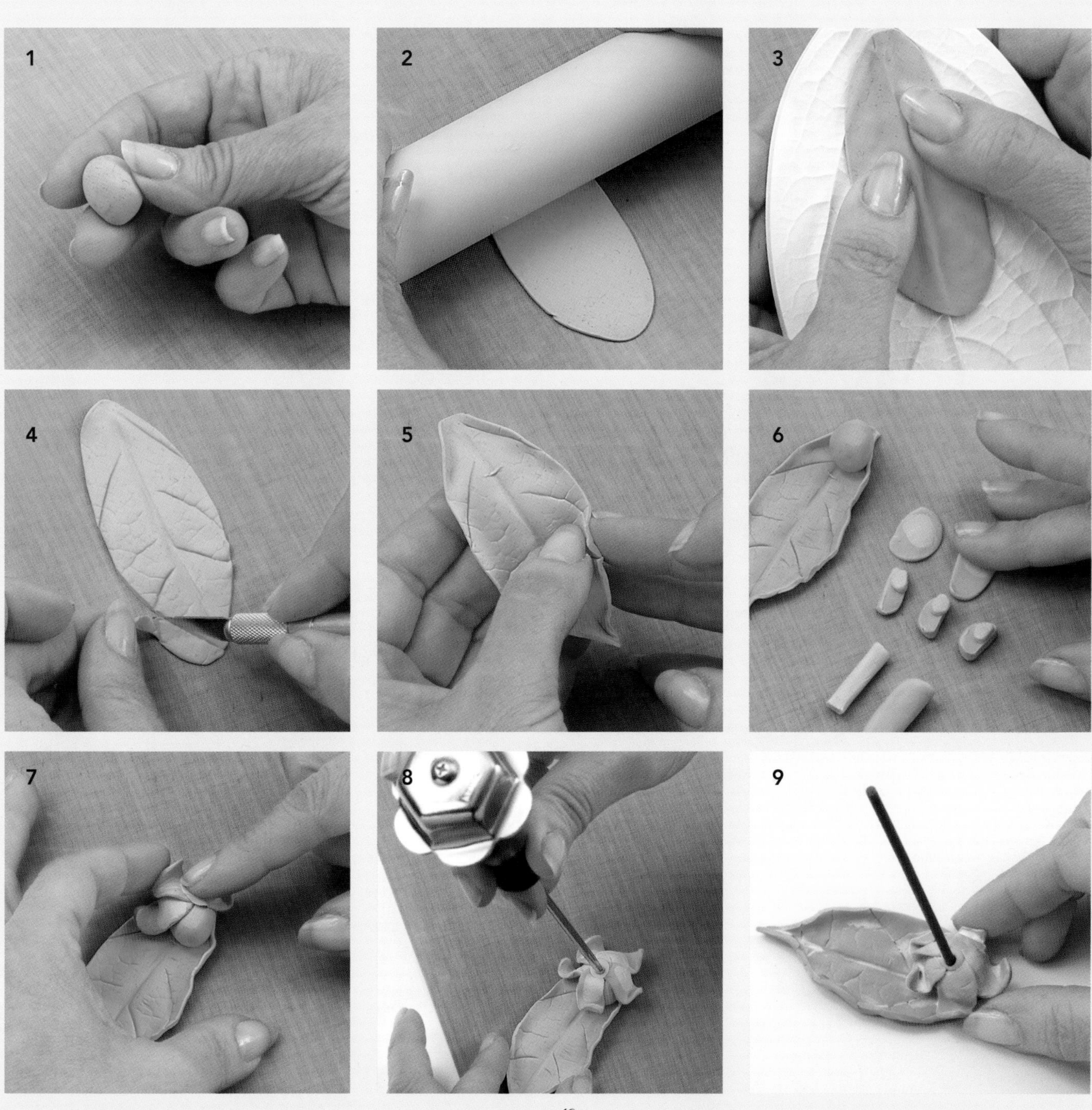

Herbes de Provence

A very traditional blend of herbs from Provence, a region in southern France, is stashed in a sweet, clear-topped, round tin for a French-themed party. This charming favor was made for a wedding shower for our friend Jessica, and it tied into the theme of her beautiful wedding. If you're making a large quantity of favors, you can purchase dried herbs in bulk at the local health food store or in large containers at warehouse stores.

Materials (per favor)

4 ounce round tin with clear top, 2⅜" diameter (see resources on page 57)

Mixed herbs (see recipe)

⅓ yard ¼" wide black and white checked ribbon

Pink label

Double-sided tape

Herbes de Provence Recipe

1 part dried thyme

1 part dried rosemary

1 part dried sage

1 part dried basil

1 part dried summer savory

1 part dried lavender buds

Mix all herbs together.

Instructions

Fill 4 ounce tins to the top with herbs. Color-photocopy the labels on page 60 (or use the information below to make your own). Wrap a label around the base of each tin. Secure the end with double-sided tape. Tie the checked ribbon around the tin, and use a piece of double-sided tape on the tin bottom to hold the ribbon in place. Finish by tying a small bow.

Herbes de Provence Label

An aromatic mixture, reflecting herbs from the Provence region in southern France. A combination of thyme, rosemary, sage, basil, summer savory, and lavender. Mix with oil and butter or use as a dry rub on meats, poultry, or fish before roasting. Divine in soups, rice, and pasta. Add a teaspoon to marinades or vinaigrette recipes. Add a pinch to hot coals for grilling. Bon appétit!

Jessica's Blend
Herbes de Provence
Add a pinch to hot coals for grilling. Bon appetit!

Citrus Scented Bath Salts

You'll love presenting these favors at a girls' beach house get-away or a summer-themed spa party set in the middle of winter. Sunny yellow, citrus scented bath salts are reminiscent of a summer breeze, and a handful dissolved in a warm bath will transport you to a toasty July day by the pool. Scoop a little at a time or use the entire tin at once for a decadent, soothing, skin smoothing bath experience.

Dead Sea salt crystals, rich in mineral salts found along the shore of the Dead Sea, are unique in character and famous for their healing and therapeutic properties. They help to relieve aches and pains, and prevent stiffness after exercising by relaxing the muscles. Epsom salt is a natural magnesium sulfate, helpful in detoxifying the skin, soothing swelling, and generally aiding the well-being of the skin.

Materials (per favor)

2½" round tin
30" hemp cording
3 frosted glass beads
Citrus scented bath salts (see resources)
1½" scallop shell
12" x 12" beach-themed two-sided patterned scrapbook paper
Double-sided tape

Instructions

Fill each tin with citrus scented bath salts to within ¼" of the top. Press a small scallop shell into the salts for scooping. Cut patterned scrapbook paper into 1¼" x 8" strips, reserving left over pieces for tags. Wrap a strip around the base of the tin and secure with double-sided tape. Alternate using either side of the patterned paper for variety on the tins. Using the hemp cord, wrap three times around the side of the lid and secure tightly with a knot. Tie glass beads onto the hemp cord tails and trim. For each tin make a small tag from the patterned paper. Add a short greeting then attach to the cord.

Scented Bath Salts Recipe

3 parts Epsom salts
2 parts baking soda
1 part table salt (Dead Sea Salts or borax)
Essential oils in either sweet orange, lavender, chamomile (works as a sedative) or sandlewood

Mix dry ingredients thoroughly using your hands. Add the essential oils, drop by drop and one at a time, until you are happy with the scent. Use your hands and fingertips to mix well.

Thea

Hidden Treasures

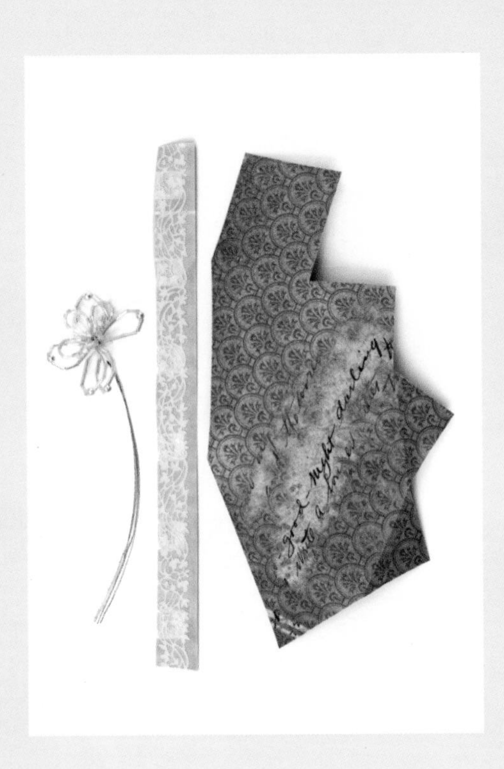

Here's a clever little pyramid-shaped box to fashion from the myriad of lovely decorative papers available these days. It's the perfect size to hold a single delicious truffle or other tiny treasure to "wow" your guests. Pick your trims to complement your paper, or if you've collected an abundance of trims, pick your paper to match the trims. Decorate tops, bottoms, or sides—anything and everything goes! Use the simple pattern to cut, score, and fold the paper then seal your treasure inside with just one piece of tape at the bottom. Simple and charming—your guests will love these fanciful little gifts.

Materials

Decorative patterned paper

Double-sided tape or paper glue

Trims and embellishments

Candy or other treats

Instructions

Trace the pattern (see page 64) onto tracing paper then transfer to the back of decorative paper. (Two will fit on a piece of 8½" x 11" paper.) Cut out and score along fold lines. If finishing the top of the point with a flower or other embellishment, adhere near the point before proceeding. Then fill with candy or other treats fold into a pyramid, and seal bottom with a piece of double-sided tape or paper glue. Glue a 1¾" square of paper to the bottom. Add feather boa trim around the bottom or gather French wired ribbon and other embellishments as shown in photos to finish off the bottom and sides of box for a fun and festive feel to match your event's theme.

B
Served
DAILY

Rose Water Glycerin Bath

With a nod to gentler Victorian times, this old fashioned, rose glycerin skin softening bath additive will be a welcomed little gift for all the women at any romantic occasion. The mixture of moisturizing glycerin and rosewood essential oil creates a soothing luxurious bath soak that guests will love. Packaged in a charming glass bottle filled with roses, your friends will truly feel pampered.

Materials (per favor)

6 ounce round bottle with cork stopper, 3" x 4¼"
Rosy bath additive (see recipe)
1" artificial roses, 4 or 5 per bottle
⅛ yard 1" wide pale pink ribbon
⅓ yard ⅛" wide pale pink ribbon
Double-sided tape
Flower-shaped paper punch
Colored paper tag

Roses Bath Recipe (per favor)

¾ cup vegetable glycerin
4 drops of rosewood essential oil
Mix both ingredients together. Rosewood essential oil is less expensive than some other rose oils and smells just as lovely. For an even more relaxing aroma, add some lavender oil. Shelf life is 4 to 8 months.

Instructions

Push the small artificial roses into the bottle. Fill the bottle with the rose mixture almost to the neck. Wrap the pink ribbon around the neck, securing the end with double-sided tape. Color -photocopy the labels on page 59 (or make your own). Cut out label and punch a small hole through one petal. Knot one end of the narrow pink ribbon then thread the pink ribbon through the hole in the label. The knot will hold the label in place. Tie the ribbon around the bottle neck, securing with a knot, then tie another knot on the opposite end.

Rosy Astringent

Instead of the rose glycerin mixture, you may want to fill your bottles with a great rosy astringent solution that can be used as a facial cleanser. For this you will need to add rose water. Purchase rose water at a health food store or make your own using dried rose petals (preferably damask roses from the health food store). Pour one cup boiling water over a cup of dried petals and seal in a jar overnight. Strain the next day, then combine 3 ounces of rose water with 3 ounces of glycerin and 4 drops of rose oil per bottle.

Rose Water
Glycerin Bath
Rose Water
Glycerin Bath
Rose Water
Glycerin Bath
Rose Water
Glycerin Bath
Rose Water
Glycerin Bath

Cranberry Lip Gloss

A big, bright daisy with a glossy, dewy cranberry lip gloss center will bring a smile to the lips of your dearest friends. These snappy favors are perfect for any springtime gathering—garden party, shower, or birthday. The daisy center contains an easy-to-make lip balm that will create a lasting impression as it is used over and over to soothe and sweeten dry lips.

Materials (per favor)

Small round plastic jar, approx. 1½" diameter (see resources)
Cranberry lip gloss filling (see recipe)
Artificial Gerbera daisy (petal layers taken apart)
2 small clear flat jewels
Glue
Colored tag

Lip Gloss Recipe (per favor)

1 tablespoon sweet almond oil
10 fresh (or frozen) cranberries
1 teaspoon honey
1 drop vitamin E oil
Small sieve and cheesecloth for straining

Using a microwave-safe bowl, mix together sweet almond oil, fresh cranberries, honey, and vitamin E oil. Microwave for two minutes or until the mixture just begins to boil. Stir well and gently crush berries. Cool mixture for five minutes, then strain through a fine sieve to remove fruit pieces. Remove liquid, using a clean piece of cheesecloth or thin cotton fabric to hold the mixture. Twist the top of the fabric closed to make a bundle and squeeze the liquid out by pressing with the back of a large spoon against the side of the sieve. Stir again and set aside to cool completely. When cool, carefully spoon into a small plastic jar. Wait an hour or so, and magically the mixture will have set up into a beautiful ruby-colored gel.

Instructions

Using parts from the artificial daisy, glue a leaf to the back of the large petal layer. Center the small petal layer on top and glue in place (see photo, right). Glue a pot of lip gloss to the daisy center then add 2 clear flat crystals to the top for dew drops. Color-photocopy the "Blow me a kiss!" tag on page 59 (or make your own). Slip the right edge under the lip balm jar and adhere with glue.

Blow me a Kiss
Cranberry Lip Balm for sweet luscious lips
Blow me a Kiss
Cranberry Lip Balm for sweet luscious lips
Blow me a Kiss
Cranberry Lip Balm for sweet luscious lips
Blow me a Kiss
Cranberry Lip Balm for sweet luscious lips

Votives for All Occasions

Designed by Debby DeBenedetti

These clever votives show that there are endless variations for creating a charming gift favor using a simple container—in this case an inexpensive glass votive holder. Using microbeads from the craft store, these holders are easy to embellish with designs to complement any theme, whether it's classy and chic or fun and whimsical. Use the ideas shown here or call upon your inner artist to customize and personalize your own creations. Add ribbons and embellishments then fill with a scented candle or colorful candy, and your guests will walk away with a welcomed treat.

Fleur de Lis Votive

Materials

Glass votives with straight sides
Assorted microbeads
Glitter
Heavy-duty double-sided tape (sheets and rolls of varying widths)
Assorted punches or die cuts
Shallow container (e.g., paper plate)
Small paint brush
Assorted ribbons, charms, tags, and embellishments
Various candles or candy to fill votives
Inkpad or decorative chalks (optional)
Glue
Adhesive dots

Instructions

Refer to the Fleur de Lis instructions below for adhering microbeads and glitter to votive holders. Use die cuts or punches and double-sided adhesive sheets to make shapes. For stripes and decorative edges, use double-sided tape in appropriate widths. To make tags, generate and print out text using a computer then center on die cuts and punch out. For an antique look, distress edges of tags by rubbing lightly on an inkpad or with decorative chalks. Some printed tags are provided on page 58 for you to color-photocopy, if you prefer.

Fleur de Lis Votive

Die cut punch the fleur de lis and flourish shapes. Remove paper backing from one side of tape and place shapes and flourishes on votive. Punch out dots from double-sided adhesive. Place adhesive dots randomly on votive, removing outside protective paper coating. Pour small gold microbeads in shallow container. Roll votive in gold beads, pressing loose beads firmly with fingers to fill sparse areas. Remove outer protective paper coating from fleur de lis and flourishes. Pour black glitter into a shallow container then roll votive in glitter. Press glitter with fingers, so it adheres to the tape shapes. Remove remaining glitter dust from votive using a paint brush. Glue gold fleur de lis charm over glittered fleur de lis. Insert tea light candle to finish.

GIVE
thanks
love
VALENTINE'S DAY
be mine
VALENTINE'S DAY
A
perfect
DAY
THANKS
freedom
celebration

Candlelight & Rosebuds

Guests will always remember your party when taking this travel candle favor along on future travels. The sweet little candle tin tucks easily into a suitcase pocket or makeup bag and will add ambience to a moonlight evening for two at the beach or a lonely hotel room during a business trip to Paris. It's filled with a scented candle and fragrant rosebuds that are sure to calm and soothe after a busy day away from home.

Materials (per favor)

2¾" diameter x 1" tall tin with clear top
Small dried pink rosebuds
Tea light candle in metal or plastic sleeve
9" of ¼" wide black ribbon with white Swiss dots
9" of ⅜" wide white ribbon with black Swiss dots
Narrow double-sided tape
Clear-drying glue or small hot glue gun and glue
Small pink silk rose with beaded center
(cut from ribbon trim)
Label for bottom of tin (see page 60)
Circle template

Instructions

Center the metal or plastic tea light holder inside the tin and hot glue in place. Cut stems off roses and make sure roses are not too large to fit in inside closed tin. Add a ring of hot glue around the holder and place dried rose buds edge-to-edge into the glue to completely encircle the holder. Wrap double-sided tape around the side of the lid and tin base then wrap with the two pieces of ribbon. Add a round label to the bottom of the tin using the "Bon Voyage" labels provided or by printing out your own message on white paper and using a circle template to cut it out. Adhere with double-sided tape. Glue a small silk rose with beaded center to top center of tin to finish off.

Seaside Bath Fizzies

The scallop sea shells in this favor look like they're filled with fresh, sparkly sand from an exotic beach. The "scooped sand" is actually baking soda and citric acid, mixed with essential oils, and soap glitter, resulting in delightful and aromatic fizzies for the bath. Whether you're celebrating a birthday, bon voyage, or seaside wedding, a charming bundle of fizzes and shells will be a hit with guests at your next beach-themed party. Later guests can relax at home in a luxurious scented bath. After dropping a fizzy into a tub filled with warm water, it will dissolve away their cares as they breathe in the lovely scent of lavender and soak in the skin softening water—a great way to relax after a stressful day at work or a strenuous day of hiking the seaside dunes.

Materials (for 8 favors)

2 dozen 1½" scallop shells
Fizzy filling (see recipe)
Assorted small sea shells
10" circle off-white tulle
1 yard raffia
Colored tag
⅛" paper punch
Decorative edge scissors

Fizzies Recipe (fills 24 shells)

1 cup citric acid (see resources)
1 cup baking soda
¼ teaspoon silver soap glitter (fine)
3 tablespoons jojoba or sweet almond oil
3 tablespoons glycerin
10 drops lavender essential oil

Mix citric acid, baking soda, and glitter together in a large bowl using a whisk. In a separate bowl mix the jojoba or almond oil with the glycerin and essential oil. Add ¼ of the liquid to the dry ingredients at a time; mix quickly with your hands until well blended. The mixture will look fluffy like snow! Working quickly, continue to add more liquid until the mixture holds together when squeezed in your fist. Time is of the essence. Press firmly into the shells, overfilling them for a mounded top. If you have some ingredients left over, put in a zip-loc bag and add a little more liquid to mold at a later time.

Instructions

When shell mixture is completely dry, package 3 fizzies with a handful of small shells to make each party favor. Place all in the center of an off-white tulle circle, gather the edges together, and secure with a raffia tie. Color-photocopy the "Bath Fizzies" Cut-out tags on page 61 (or make your own cut out) with decorative edge scissors (or make your own), punch a hole at the left end, then add to the raffia tie.

Tell guests to drop the entire tulle bag into the bathtub (remove tag first) and watch it turn into lovely aromatic sea foam. After the fizzing has stopped, they can remove the bag and save the shells to display. Or, for three times the fun, they can open the bag and add just one fizzy, saving the rest to savor on another day.

Beach Party
BATH FIZZIES
Beach Party
BATH FIZZIES
Beach Party
BATH FIZZIES
Beach Party
BATH FIZZIES

Think Outside the Box

A cross between crackerjack prizes and fortune cookies, these little affirmations or positive words of encouragement are meant to inspire introspection, change, and action on the part of the recipient. Present to guests at a 40th, 50th or other "decade" birthday party, a graduation, or some other life changing or milestone celebration. Getting "real" is in, so have your guests read these aloud and express what the words might mean to them in their personal lives.

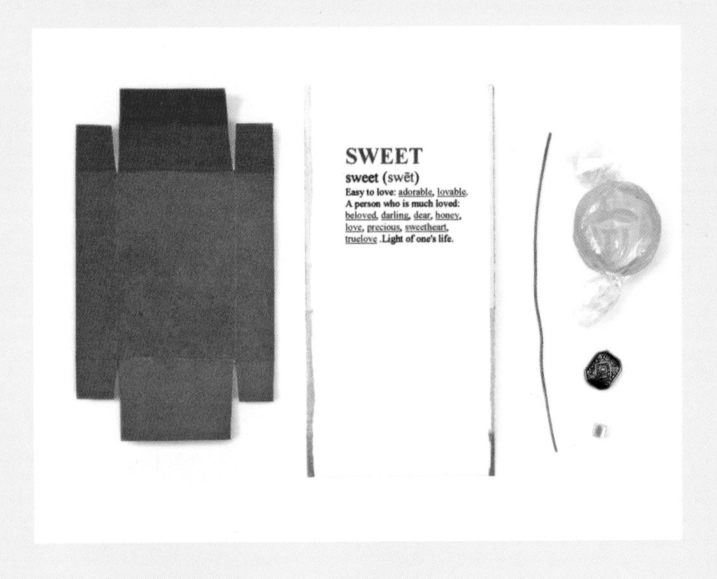

Materials (for 10 favors)

Tracing paper
12" x 12" sheet double-sided heavy scrapbook paper
8½" x 11" white card stock
Bone folder
Double-sided tape
Gold leafing marker
Sharp needle
20-gauge copper wire
Wire cutters
Needle nose pliers
Medium sized beads
1½" pinback (optional)

Instructions

Trace pattern for box base on page 61 onto tracing paper and transfer to double-sided decorative paper; cut out. See tips for transferring on page 61. Score with a bone folder as indicated. To form box, fold sides (2) up and tabs (1) in, then fold ends (3) up and fold over ends (4) on score line to overlap tabs on inside of box. Adhere with double-sided tape. For the outer sleeve cut 2" x 4¼" rectangles from white card stock and score following lines on outer sleeve template on page 61. Color-photocopy the dictionary definitions on page 39 onto white card stock and cutout just the inside of black outline. (If you prefer, use a computer to make your own affirmations. Use colors to complement the paper design of your box and leave enough white space around your definition to cut out the 2" x 4¼" outer sleeve shape.)

carefully and at leng
consider, contemplate,
mull, muse, ponder,
BLOOM
bloom (blūm)
verb. To grow rapidly and luxuriantly: blossom, flourish, flower, thrive.
DEPTH
depth (dĕpth)
noun. The condition or quality of being deep. The most profound or intense part or stage. Inten force: had not realized the d of their feelings for one another
HARMONY
har·mo·ny (här' mə-nē)
Agreement in feeling or opinion; accord: live in harmony. A pleasing
MOVE
move (mūv)
verb. To go forward, towar conclusion: advance, progress. To stir to act feeling: inflame,
EXPLORE
ex·plore (ĭk-splôr', -splōr') verb. To go into for the purpose of making discoveries or acquiring information: delve, dig, inquire, investigate, look into.
FLY
(flī)
To engage in fligh
through the air by the wind:
kite flying above the playgro
verb To feel devoted love for: adore, See love/hatred. To like or enjoy enthusiastically, often excessively: adore, delight (in),
LEAP
leap (lēp)
To spring or bound
leaped over
desire or
desire,
will. See
a strong longing
desire.
COMMIT
com·mit (kə-mĭt')
verb. To put in the charge of another for care, use, or performance: commend, confide, consign, entrust, give (over
JOURN
jour·ney
verb. A process or c
to traveling; a passage:
journey of life. travel, trek,
hit the road. make one's

Accent each long edge of sleeve, using a gold leafing marker. Starting at the top of the sleeve, score at ½", 1⅞", 2⅜", and 3¾" as shown on pattern, then fold on score lines. Use double-sided tape to adhere ends together. Cut out affirmation and glue to top of sleeve.

Use a sharp needle to punch a hole in one short side of box for drawer pull. Cut a 1¼" piece of wire. Form a loop on one end using needle nose pliers. Add three medium sized beads, then use the pliers to secure beads on wire with another loop. Fill each match box with a little prize that illustrates the word on the outside. Refer to the "treasure list" below for ideas. Possibly add a pinback to wear or just place in a low bowl for your guests to choose as little prizes like those found in the treasure chest at the dentist's office or in a box of crackerjacks!

Reflect – mirror
Commit – ring
Love – heart
Bloom – rose
Sparkle – jewel
Sweet – candy
Explore – compass
Journey – plane
Move – car
Wish – fairy
Wisdom – Smarties candy
Fly – bird/lady bug
Hug – bear
Leap – frog
Harmony – harmonica
Depth – fish
Play – game
Expand – balloon
The list could go on and on with a little imagination and few tiny toys!

BLOOM
bloom (blūm)
verb. To grow rapidly and luxuriantly: blossom, flourish, flower, thrive.

COMMIT
com·mit (kə-mĭt')
verb. To put in the charge of another for care, use, or performance: commend, confide, consign, entrust.

DEPTH
depth (dĕpth)
noun. The condition or quality of being deep. The most profound or intense part or stage. Intensity; force: *had not realized the depth of their feelings for one another*.

EXPAND
ex·pand (ĭk-spănd')
verb. To make or become greater or larger: aggrandize, amplify, boost, build up, enlarge, escalate, extend, grow, increase, magnify, multiply, proliferate, rise.

EXPLORE
ex·plore (ĭk-splôr')
verb. To go into for the purpose of making discoveries or acquiring information: delve, dig, inquire, investigate, look into.

FLY
fly (flī)
v.intr. To engage in flight, to move through the air by means of wings. To rise in or be carried through the air by the wind: *a kite flying above the playground.*

HARMONY
har·mo·ny (här'mə-nē)
noun. Agreement in feeling or opinion; accord: *live in harmony.* A pleasing combination of elements in a whole: *the order and harmony of the universe.*

HUG
hug (hŭg)
v.tr. To clasp or hold closely, as in affection; embrace. To hold steadfastly to; cherish: *He still hugs his outmoded beliefs.*

JOURNEY
jour·ney (jûr'nē)
verb. A process or course likened to traveling; a passage: *the journey of life.* travel, trek, trip. hit the road. make one's way.

LEAP
leap (lēp)
verb. To spring or bound upward; jump: *leaped over the wall.* An abrupt or precipitous passage, shift, or transition: *a leap from rags to riches.*

LOVE
love (lŭv)
verb. To feel deep, devoted love for: adore, worship. *See* love/hatred
To like or enjoy enthusiastically, oftenexcessively: adore, delight (in).

MOVE
move (mūv)
verb. To go forward, toward a conclusion: advance, proceed, progress. To stir to action or feeling: inflame, inspire, prompt.

PLAY
play (plā)
verb. To occupy oneself in amusement, sport, or other recreation: *children playing with toys.* To move or seem to move quickly, lightly: *The breeze played on the water.*

REFLECT
re·flect (rĭ-flĕkt')
verb. To think or think about carefully and at length: cogitate, consider, contemplate, meditate, mull, muse , ponder.

SPARKLE
spar·kle (spär'kəl)
verb. A glittering quality. Too shine with animation. To sparkle with with brilliant animation; vivacity.

SWEET
sweet (swēt)
adj. Easy to love: adorable, lovable. A person who is much loved: beloved, darling, dear, honey, love, precious, sweetheart, truelove. Light of one's life.

WISDOM
wis·dom (wĭz'dəm)
noun. The ability to discern or judge what is true, right, or lasting; insight.

WISH
wish (wĭsh)
verb. To have the desire or inclination to: choose, desire, like[1], please, want, will. *See* desire. To have a strong longing for: ache, covet, desire.

Mardi Gras Cajun Spices

This Cajun inspired dry rub blend of seasonings would be the perfect addition to a Mardi-gras-themed party. "Laissez les bon temps roulez," i.e., "let the good times roll," sets the tone for this spicy little gift that guests can enjoy at home when grilling, roasting, and sautéing. Use this savory mixture to fill small salt and pepper shakers from a restaurant supply, import store, or discount store. Add purple beads, gold twist tie ribbon, and a zippy label to complete this hot little number.

Materials

Salt and pepper shakers (see resources)
Cajun spiced salt (see recipe)
Purple mardi gras beads
Gold twist tie ribbon
Pencil
Colored paper label
Double-sided tape

Cajun Spiced Salt Recipe

3 parts salt
1 part granulated garlic
1 part fine black pepper
1 part fine red pepper
1 part paprika
1 part fine oregano
Combine all ingredients and mix well.

Instructions

Fill containers with Cajun seasonings then finish off with gold and purple sparkly accents. For each shaker cut a 3" piece of purple beads and a 12" piece of gold twist tie ribbon. Twist the ribbon tightly around the neck of the shaker, attaching the beads at the same time. Wrap the ends of the ribbon around a pencil to make the curls. Color-photocopy the labels on page 59 (or make your own) and attach diagonally using double-sided tape.

Include a printed card with ingredients and suggestions on how to use this delicious spicy mixture. The seasoning can be used as a dry rub for grilled, roasted, sautéed, or blackened meat, poultry, fish or vegetables. It's also great in sauces, marinades, gravy, or mixed into pasta salads and more to add that Louisiana taste to almost any savory dish.

Mardi Gras Cajun
Laissez les bon temps roulez –
NEW ORLEANS

Swing Into Spring

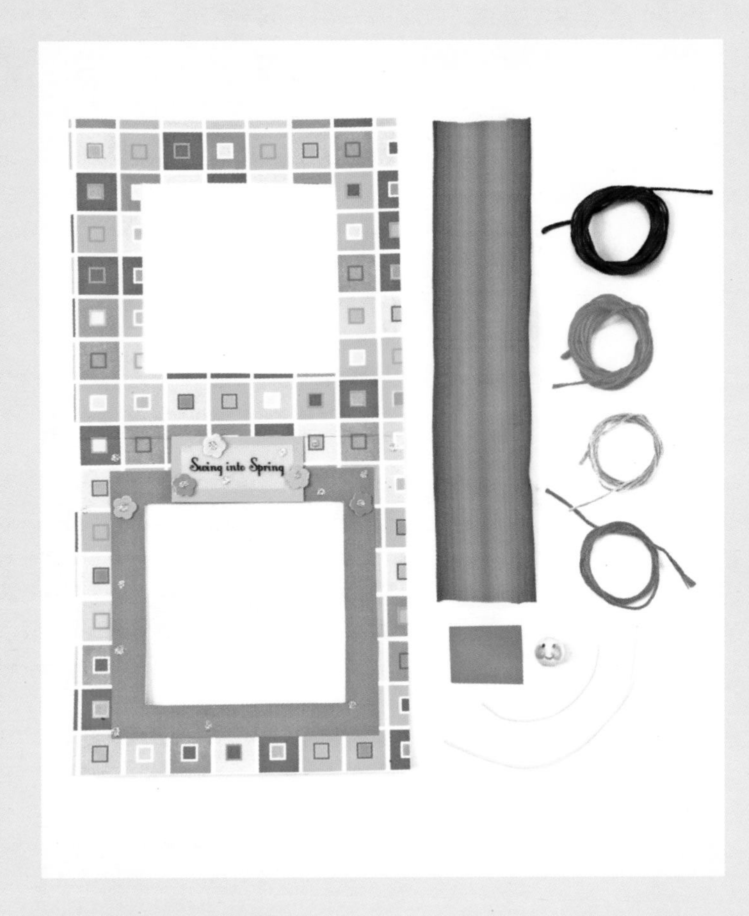

Designed by Gina Gabriell

Lighthearted and fun, these swinging fairies are sure to tickle the heartstrings of your guests. They swing freely in the tented card opening and will add a touch of whimsy to a desktop, mantel, bookcase, or table while catching the breeze. It's easy to remove the little fairy doll from the card to decorate a tassel, pencil topper, barrette, or pinback. She also makes a lovable plaything in a little girl's fantasy world. Made of floral wire, a wooden bead head, and bits of ribbon and embroidery floss, these delightful little sprites will keep everyone smiling.

Materials

Card

- Tracing paper
- Colored and patterned papers
- ¼" flower punch
- Paper glue
- Fine glitter
- Velum paper for printed tags
- Labels

Fairy

- White floral wire (cloth covered wire spool)
- 12mm wooden bead for head
- Colored pencils or watercolors with small brush
- 1½" wide ribbon
- Embroidery floss in three colors
- Needle and thread
- Small hot glue gun and glue

Swing into Spring

Swing into Spring

Swing into Spring

Swing into Spring

Swing into Spring

Swing into Spring

Swing into Spring

Swing into Spring

Swing into Spring

Instructions

Card

Trace the patterns for the card base shape and smaller frame layer (see page 63) onto tracing paper. Transfer to the back of two coordinating pieces of decorative paper and cut out. Also punch out flowers to embellish card using assorted colored papers. Score fold of card with bone folder and fold in half. Use paper glue to layer card base and smaller frame together. Photocopy onto velum paper the "Swing Into Spring" labels on page 59 (or make your own) and cut out. Cut a 1⅞" x ⅞" rectangle from colored paper. Use paper glue to adhere the "Swing Into Spring" label to the colored rectangle then glue to top center front of card. Glue flower punches to card as shown. Use small dots of paper glue and fine glitter to add sparkle dots and centers to flowers for extra pizzazz.

Fairy

To make the fairy's body, cut a 4" piece of floral wire and also a 2" piece. Fold the longer piece in half and wrap the shorter piece to it, starting about ¼" down from the fold [photo 1]. Cut a 7" piece of 1½" ribbon (if using wired ribbon, slip the wires out and discard). Use a needle and thread to run a basting stitch along one long edge of ribbon [photo 2]. Pull the thread tight and tie ends together to make the full skirt for the fairy [photo 3].

Draw the face (mouth, eyes, cheeks) onto the wooden bead with colored pencils or watercolors and a fine brush [photo 4]. Make the hair by looping 1 yard of embroidery floss in desired color around three fingers and tying loosely in the middle with matching floss [photo 5]. Hot glue hair to the wooden bead by applying a small amount to the top of the head and pressing hair down on top. Add more glue around the sides of head and press hair down [photo 6]. For fun, customize each hairstyle to make buns, ponytails, etc. so that each card is unique! Add a small bow or floss headband to finish hair.

Using 1 yard of floss to match the ribbon dress, start wrapping floss at fairy's waist (about ¼" below attached arms), leaving a 1" tail to tie off later. Wrap floss around the torso and arms. Leave ¼" of the wire exposed at the end of each arm to make a small hook when finished. Continue wrapping down the torso and tie off at the waist using the tail where you began [photo 7].

Assemble all parts using a hot glue gun. Glue the head on by slipping the hole of the bead over the top of the "neck" [photo 8]. Glue the skirt on underneath to secure [photo 9]. Fold in ⅛" on each end of the floral wire arms so she can hold onto her swing. If you wish, here is where you can add small flowers, wings, or little crowns to your fairy, using bits of velum paper, small feathers, or short pieces of gold trim. The sky's the limit for dressing up these little girls.

Make a swing for the fairy to sit upon using a ⅞" long x 1" wide piece of card stock. Fold in half lengthwise and glue an 8" piece of tan floss into the fold equaling out the ends [photo 10]. Hook the floss ends into the fairy's hands about ½" from the swing edge and tape or hot glue into the top inside corners of the card [photo 11]. Trim ends and watch her swing into spring [photo 12]!

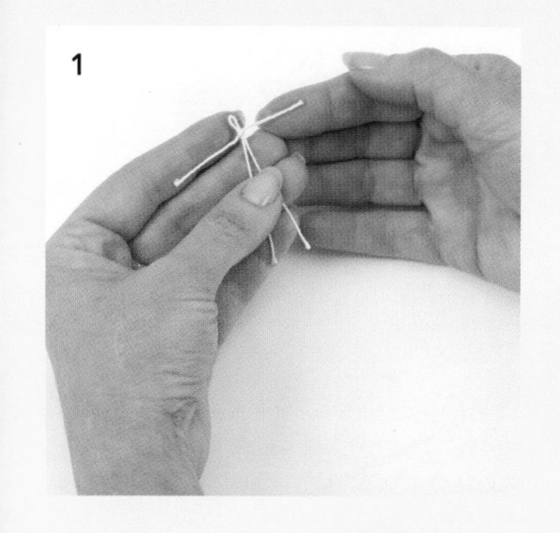
1

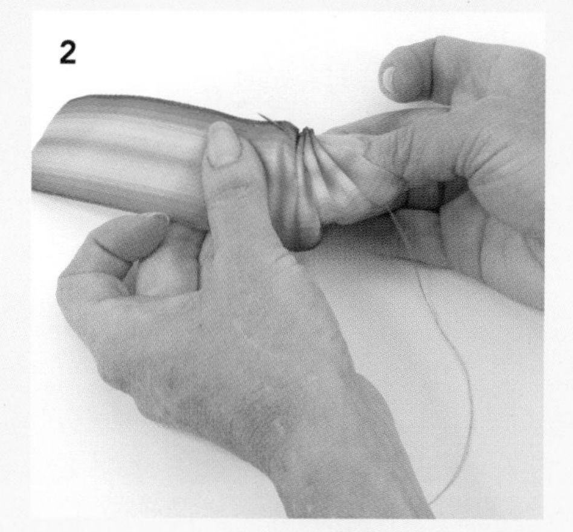
2

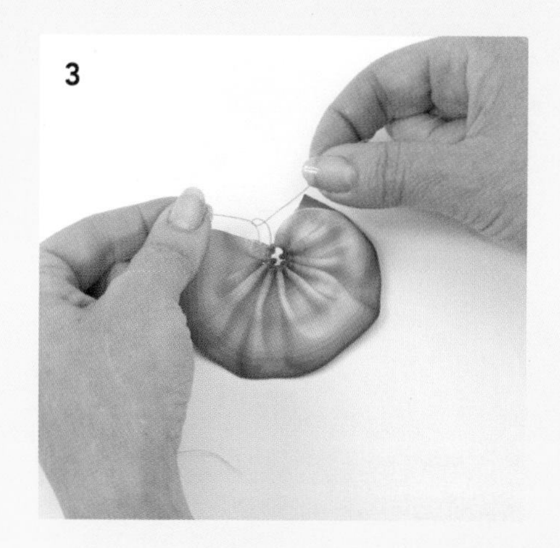
3

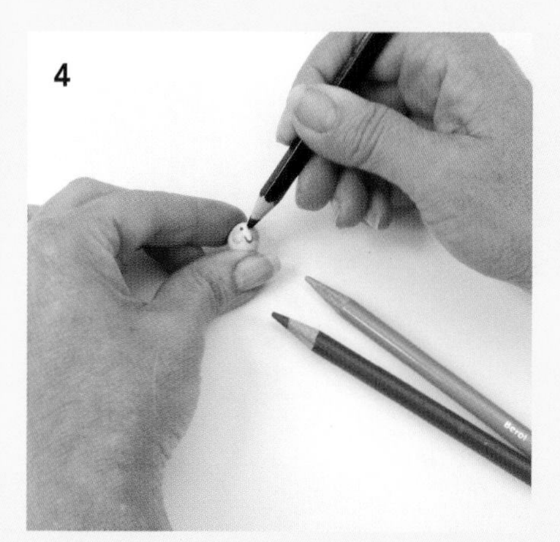
4

5

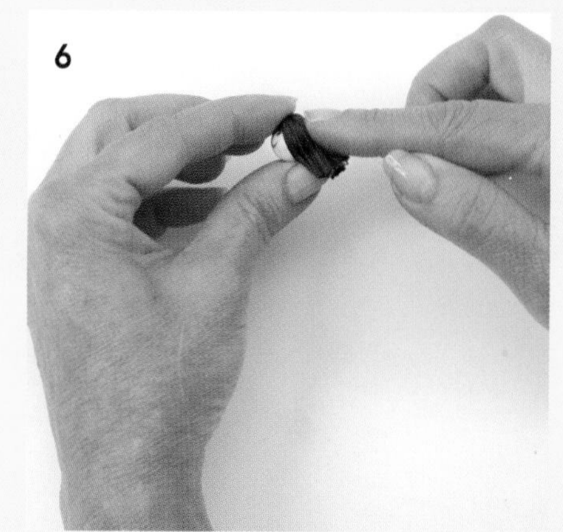
6

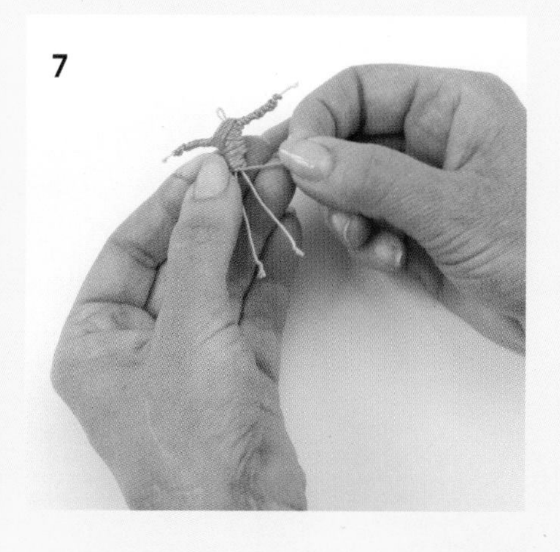
7

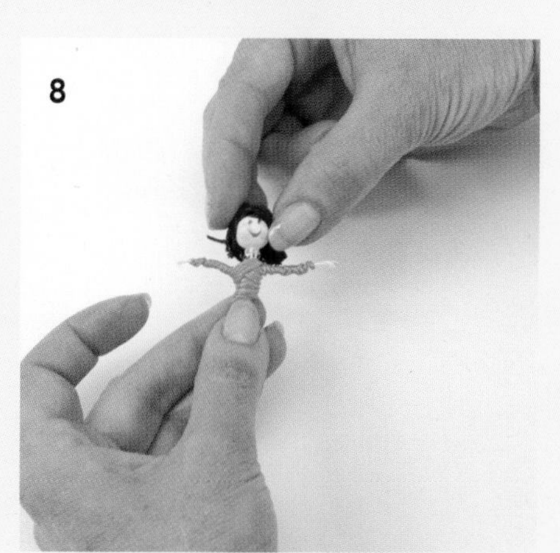
8

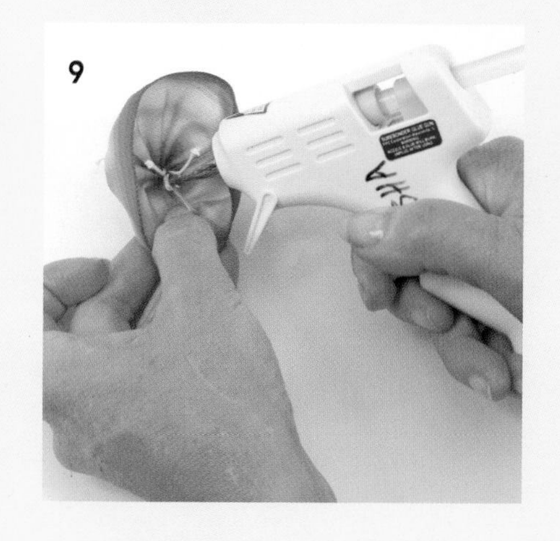
9

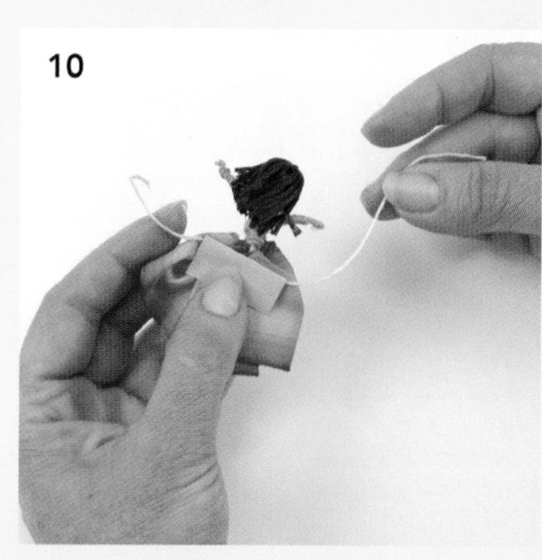
10

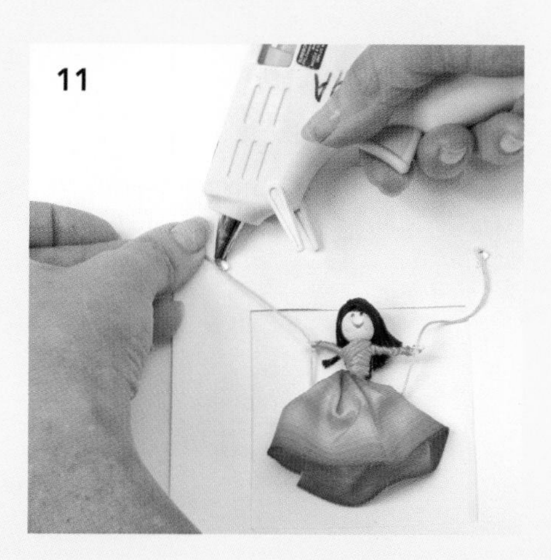
11

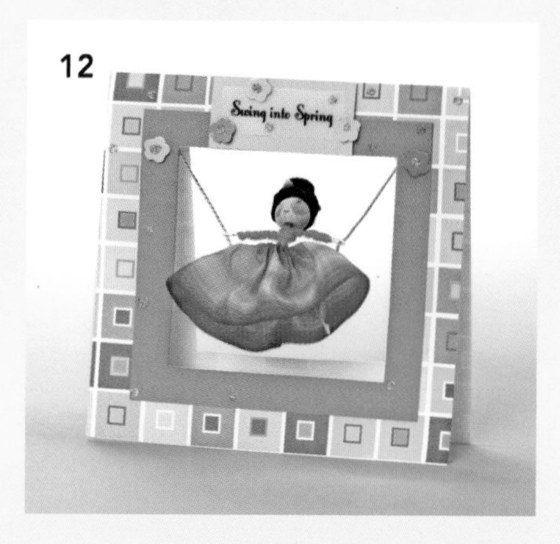
12
Swing into Spring

Purses With Pizzazz

These little purses win the prize for being the most clever and cute. They're made with everyday mint tins, so it's a fun way to recycle those tins you may have accumulated. The same silver microbeads decorate all of the purses to create three unique looks. The idea is simple—the result is charming.

1

1. Chic Stripes Purse

Materials

Candy mint tin, 3¾" x 2⅜" x ⅞"

Light blue metal paint

Awl or ice pick

18-gauge wire

Silver barrel beads, blue and clear beads

⅓ yard black polka-dot ribbon

Decorative silver clasp

.5mm silver microbeads

Paper plate

Small hot glue gun and glue

Double-sided adhesive sheets

Pliers

Chic Stripes Purse (Continued)

Instructions

Paint the entire tin (front, back, and sides) with light blue metal paint; let dry. Avoid the area where the lid overlaps the tin. Using an awl or ice pick, punch two holes on the side opposite from the hinge (see photo). For the silver stripes, cut ½" wide strips from a double-sided adhesive sheet. Apply the strips to the front, back, and sides of the tin by removing one side of the backing and spacing evenly on the tin as shown. Peel off the remaining backing and pour .5mm silver microbeads onto the adhesive, catching the excess on a paper plate. Press beads down with fingers. Add a decorative silver clasp to the front of the lid using hot glue. Add a piece of black polka-dot ribbon around the side of the lid using double-sided adhesive tape or hot glue. For the handle cut an 8" length of 18-gauge wire; add a silver barrel bead, blue bead then alternating clear and blue beads. End with a blue bead and silver barrel bead. Run the wire through the top holes and cut wire ends to about ½". Make a loop inside the tin with pliers to secure the wire handle to the tin.

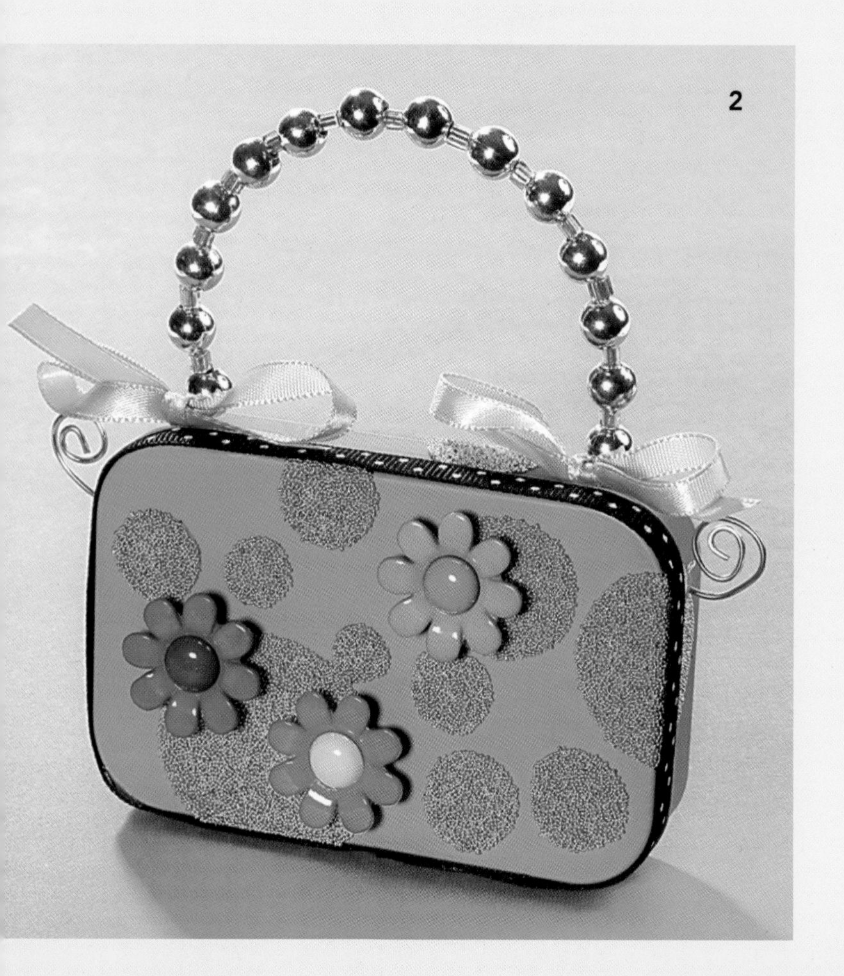

2. Flower Power Purse

Materials

Candy mint tin, 3¾" x 2⅜" x ⅞"
Light aqua metal paint
Awl or ice pick
18-gauge wire
Silver and clear beads
3 flower buttons
Wire cutters
⅓ yard black polka-dot ribbon
.5mm silver microbeads
Paper plate
Small hot glue gun and glue
Double-sided adhesive sheets
½ yard ¼" lavender satin ribbon

Instructions

Paint the entire tin with light aqua metal paint; let dry. Avoid the area where the lid overlaps the tin. Using an awl or ice pick, punch four holes in the sides of the tin—two holes on top and two on the side for attaching the wire handle (see photo). Using a circle template or coins, draw circles of various sizes on the backing of a sheet of double-sided adhesive and cut out. Apply the circles to the tin by removing one side of the backing, overlapping some of the edges and folding over onto the sides. Peel off the remaining backing and pour .5mm silver microbeads onto the adhesive, catching the excess on a paper plate. Press beads down with fingers. Remove the button shank on the back of three flower buttons using wire cutters and attach to the front of the lid with hot glue. Add a piece of black polka-dot ribbon around the side of the lid using double-sided adhesive tape or hot glue. For the handle cut a 12" length of 18-gauge wire and thread alternating silver and clear beads. Run the wire through the holes in the top of the tin and out the side holes. Cut wire ends, leaving about 2", then curl into a spiral. Add two lavender ribbon bows to the handle.

3

3. Harlequin Diamonds Purse

Materials

Candy mint tin, 3¾" x 2⅜" x ⅞"
Lavender metal paint
Awl or ice pick
18-gauge wire
.5mm silver microbeads
Paper plate
Flat acrylic jewels (assorted pink/purple colors)
Silver barrel beads, crystals, and assorted beads
Decorative silver button
Clear tacky glue
Small hot glue gun and glue
Double-sided adhesive sheets
Pliers

Instructions

Paint the entire tin with lavender metal paint; let dry. Avoid the area where the lid overlaps the tin. Using an awl or ice pick, punch two holes in the side of the tin (see photo). Using the pattern (see page 61), draw diamond shapes on the backing of a sheet of double-sided adhesive and cut out. Apply diamond shapes in the pattern as shown in the photo, starting in the center of the tin and working outward. Apply to front, back, and two sides. Peel off the remaining backing and pour .5mm silver microbeads onto the adhesive, catching the excess on a paper plate. Press beads down with fingers. Add small dots of clear glue where diamonds intersect and adhere flat acrylic jewels. Let dry and repeat on the back and sides of the tin. Add a decorative silver button to the lid using hot glue. Cut an 8" length of 18-gauge wire and thread on a silver barrel bead, then add alternating beads and crystals to the wire. Run the wire through the top holes. Cut wire ends to about ½". Make a loop inside the tin with pliers to secure the wire handle to the tin.

Terra Cotta Magnets

Perky dotted terra cotta pots with tiny, frosted artificial flowers are a sweet reminder of a great party. These little thank you gifts are useful as well as cute. The magnet on the back will anchor family snapshots and shopping lists for easy viewing on the fridge. Substitute a tiny orchid, poinsettia, or other seasonal flower to match any theme.

Materials (per favor)

1¼" diameter mini clay pot
Light pink acrylic paint
Pencil with eraser
1" diameter ball of paper clay (see resources)
Small amount of green reindeer moss
3 frosted artificial crocus flowers or similar small flowers
Hot glue gun and glue
½" diameter magnet
Colored label

Instructions

Paint pots with light pink polka dots by dipping the eraser end of a pencil in paint then dabbing randomly all around. Let dry. Roll some paper clay, into a small ball (this lightweight material won't add extra weight to the magnet). Put a dab of hot glue inside the clay pot, drop in the ball of paper clay and press down. Trim off flower stems to 1½" or less. Poke stems into the paper clay in the center of the pot. Apply more hot glue around the base of the flowers and add small pieces of reindeer moss to hide the paper clay. Hot glue the magnet to the back side of the pot. Color-photocopy the small "Thank you!" tags on page 59 (or create your own tags). Cut out tags and glue to the back of each pot just above the magnet so they resemble small banners.

Thank you!
Thank you!
Thank you!
Thank you!
Thank you!

Haute Couture

Designed by Gina Gabriell

Delightful little purses just beg to be opened! Inside you can stash candy, potpourri, tiny treasures, or even keys to the new Jaguar for an unforgettable surprise! Use coordinating papers and embellishments to match any theme or occasion and your party table will dance with color. Not just for parties, use your imagination to see how fun and versatile these tiny containers can be. They're great for wrapping a single small gift for a special friend. Or, enlarge the pattern for gift card holder ornaments to hang on the Christmas tree. This inexpensive favor is quick and easy to make whether you need oodles or just a few.

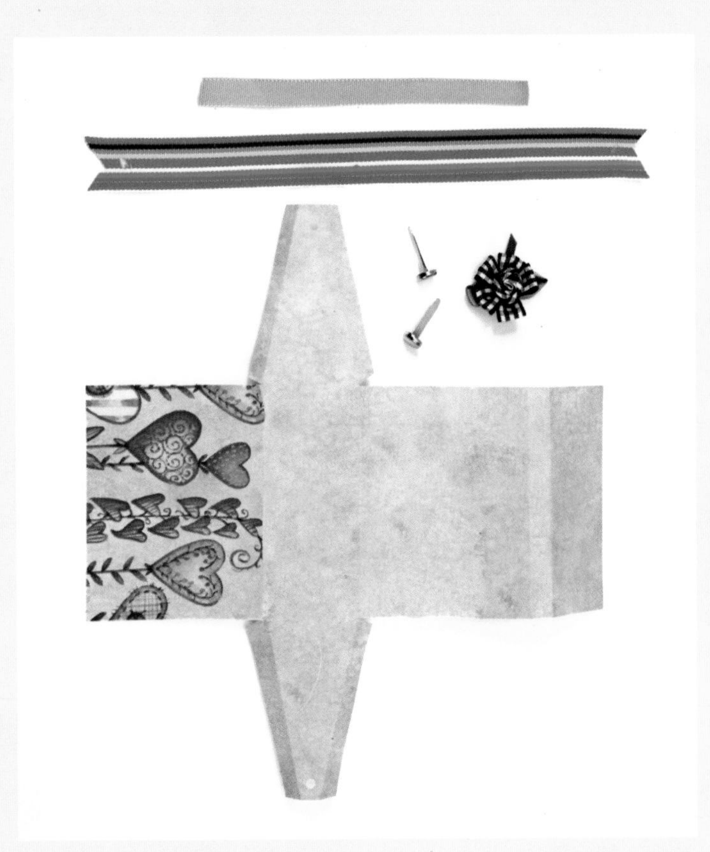

Materials (per favor)

Tracing paper
8" x 8" piece of decorative paper
Bone folder
Large needle
8" piece of ribbon for handle
Double-sided tape or paper glue
Two brads (optional)
4" piece of ribbon to trim purse flap
Fabric flower, beads, rhinestones, or other embellishments

Instructions

Trace pattern (see page 62) onto tracing paper and transfer to back of decorative paper, including fold lines; cut out. Use a bone folder to score along fold lines then fold. Use a large needle to poke holes for the purse handle as indicated on pattern. With scored edges folded to the inside, apply double-sided tape or paper glue to form the purse shape. Trim ends of ribbon handle with a "V" and attach using brads to poke first through the ribbon (about ½" from each end) then through holes in paper. Secure by opening brads on the inside (you may need to bend one end in half if it extends over the paper edge). For another method, just poke ends of ribbon through holes in paper and glue down to inside of purse. Add ribbon trim across flap along the edge, folding raw edges of ribbon to the inside. Add small embellishments to complement design (see photos). Fill as desired.

happy
birthday

Princess Tea Party

Designed by María Parrish

Sweeter than a tray stacked with petit fours, these teeny, strawberry-topped layer cakes will be a hit with both little and big girls alike. Present them to guests at your princess's Strawberry Shortcake Party or your niece's bridal shower tea. The mini cakes will serve as sweet reminders of your special day. They can dangle from a backpack, lunch box, cell phone, or purse, or make "yummy" charms and pendants for jewelry. They're so easy and fun to make, you may want to bake up a batch this weekend for your friends. Why wait for a party!

Materials (for 6 favors)

Four 2 ounce packages of polymer clay: pink, dark brown, green, red (see resources)
⅝" daisy cookie cutter
Non-stick craft sheet
Pen
Cake decorating tip to make swirl
Toothpick
Cell phone ornament cord (also called mobile strap/ lanyard); 3 red, 3 pink
Wire cutters
Needle nose pliers
¾" eyepins
Acrylic clay roller
Clay glaze or clear nail polish (optional)

Instructions

Cake: Remove a portion of the light pink clay from the package and knead in your hands for a minute. This necessary step is called "conditioning" the clay. If the clay feels flexible and can be pulled easily without breaking immediately, it is ready to go. Roll into a 1" diameter ball then use the clay roller to roll the ball into a sheet. Use the cookie cutter to cut out 2 daisies [photo 1, page 56]. Repeat using brown clay and cutting out 3 daisies. Starting with brown, stack all 5 of the daisy cutouts, alternating colors [photo 2, page 56].

Frosting: Drop another piece of pink clay inside the cake decorating tip (make sure it is well conditioned so that it is easier to extrude). Work the clay through the tip with the back of a pen until you get a 3" long swirled roll [photo 3, page 56]. Cut off a ⅝" piece and reserve the rest [photo 4, page 56]. Join the ends of the short piece to make a donut. Center it on top of the cake stack.

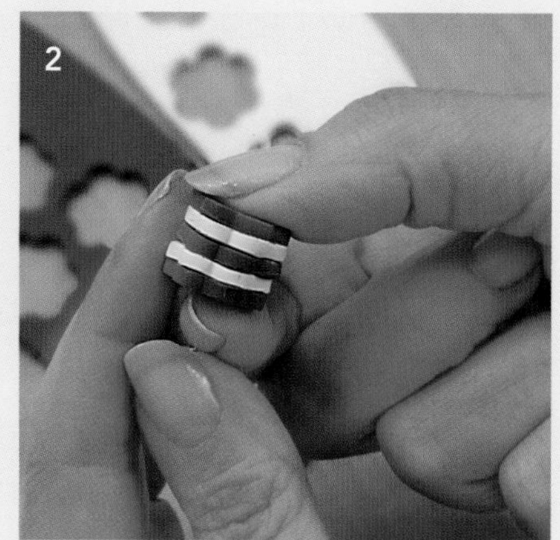

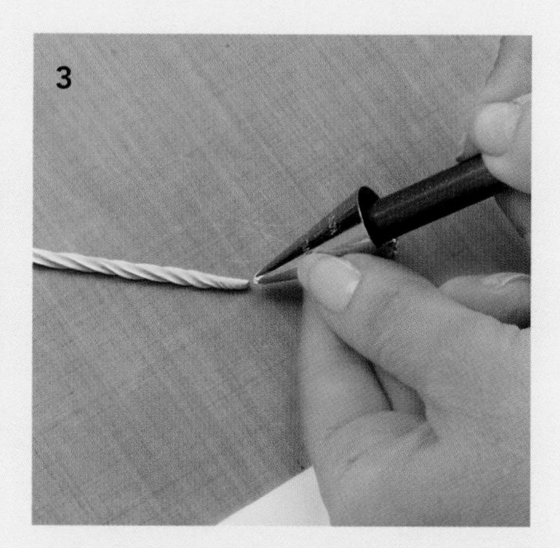

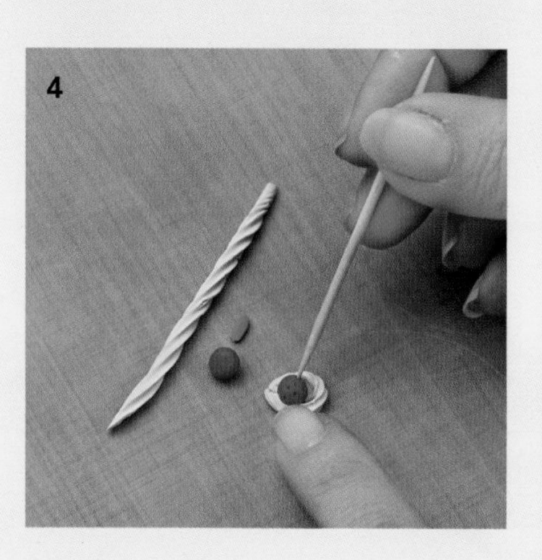

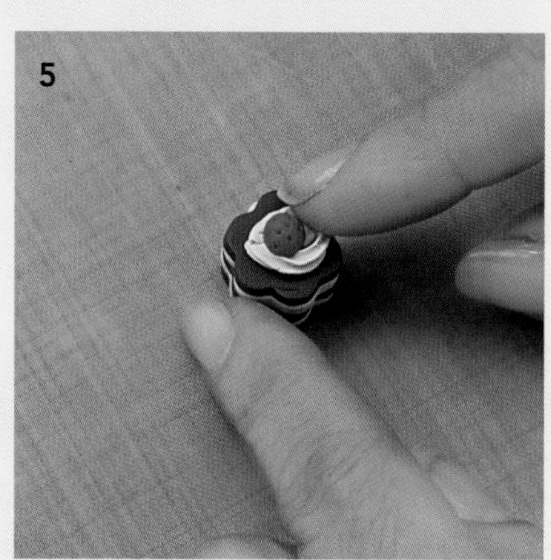

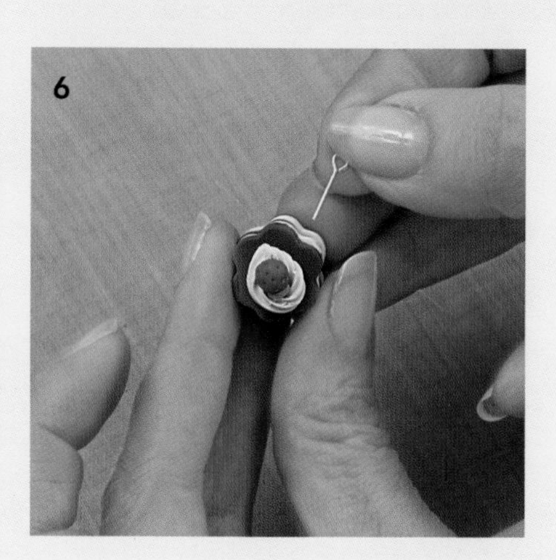

Strawberry: Make a ¼" ball of red clay and shape like a strawberry. Make a tiny leaf using the green clay and place on top of the strawberry. Add little seed dots to the strawberry using a toothpick. Then place the strawberry on top of the pink swirl [photo 5].

Finishing: Use the wire cutters to trim the eyepin to measure ½" long. Insert into the side of your cake through the center chocolate layer [photo 6]. Bake in oven at 275 degrees F (130 degrees C) for 15 minutes per quarter inch of thickness. DO NOT MICROWAVE. Let cool for 30 minutes. When cool you may choose to add a glaze. Use clay glaze or your favorite clear nail polish. Glitter nail polish will add extra sparkle. Attach the O-ring on the cell phone lanyard to the eyepin using needle nose pliers.

Tips

- If you want your cake to look spongy, use sandpaper to add texture.
- If you don't have an acrylic roller, you can use a pasta machine or water glass.
- If you can't find a cell phone lanyard, you can create your own using ribbon, beading cord, or keychain.

Espresso Yourself (page 10)
Tins from Specialty Bottle Company
service@specialtybottle.com
5200 4th Avenue South, Seattle, WA 98108
(206) 340-0459, fax: 1 206 903-0785

Bee My Honey (page 12)
Bee pin from Kooler Design Studio
www.koolerdesign.com

Kung Hey Fat Choy (page 14)
Sculpey III Clay – 2 ounce packages: Lime Green #521,
Turquoise #505, Red Hot Red #583, Glow-in-the-dark Light
Orange from Sculpey Glow-in-the-dark kit #K34064 or
mix equal parts of Atomic Orange #533 + White #001
14" clay roller from www.claycompany.com
Non-stick craft sheet or other non-stick surface from
MeltArt TM www.rangerink.com
Faux glazing medium from DecoArt

Incense Burner (page 17)
Sculpey III Clay – 2 ounce packages: Lime Green #521,
White #001, Glow-in-the-dark Light Green, Hot Pink #503,
Atomic Orange #533, Lemon #573
Leaf mold and 14" clay roller from www.claycompany.com
Non-stick craft sheet or other non-stick surface from
MeltArt TM www.rangerink.com
Faux glazing medium from DecoArt
www.decoart.com

Herbes de Provence (page 20)
4 ounce round tin from Specialty Bottle Company
service@specialtybottle.com
5200 4th Avenue South, Seattle, WA 98108
(206) 340-0459, fax: 1 206 903-0785

Citrus Scented Bath Salts (page 22)
Bath salts from My Daisy Garden,
www.mydaisygarden.com (614) 395-0321
Tins from Specialty Bottle Supply
service@specialtybottle.com
5200 4th Avenue South, Seattle, WA 98108
(206) 340-0459, fax: 1 206 903-0785

Cranberry Lip Gloss (page 28)
Small round plastic jar from Tap Plastics
www.tapplastics.com

Candlelight & Rosebuds (page 32)
Tins from Specialty Bottle Company
service@specialtybottle.com
5200 4th Avenue South, Seattle, WA 98108
(206) 340-0459, fax: (206) 903-0785

Seaside Bath Fizzies (page 34)
Citric acid from Wholespice
www.wholespice.com (415) 472-1750

Mardi Gras Cajun Spices (page 40)
Salt and pepper shakers from Ikea
www.ikea.com
Ingredients available at wholespice.com
(415) 472-1750

Terra Cotta Magnets (page 50)
Paper clay from mountain Idea
www.themountainidea.com
16920 South Main Street,
Gardena, CA 90248, (888) 900-2677

Princess Tea Party (page 54)
Sculpey III Clay – 2 ounce packages: Chocolate 053,
Ballerina 1209, Lime 521, Red Hot Red 583
5/8" Daisy cookie cutter by Wilton
Darice cell phone ornament cords #1989-29
Sculpey Glaze- Gloss Item No. ASG33G - 1.2 fl. oz (33 ml)
14" clay roller from www.claycompany.com
Non-stick craft sheet or other non-stick surface from
MeltArt TM www.rangerink.com
Faux glazing medium from DecoArt
www.decoart.com

Other Supplies
Beacon Adhesives
Customer Service, 1 800 865-7238, Mt. Vernon, New York
www.beacon1.com

Espresso Yourself!
Coffee & Brown Sugar Body Scrub
• • • • • • • • • • • • • • •
Contains: coffee, brown sugar, sweet almond oil,
essential oils of orange and lemon.
To use: open pores in a steaming shower,
vigorously massage entire body,
avoiding the face and neck area,
and rinse with warm water and feel like new!

Espresso Yourself!
Coffee & Brown Sugar Body Scrub
• • • • • • • • • • • • • • •
Contains: coffee, brown sugar, sweet almond oil,
essential oils of orange and lemon.
To use: open pores in a steaming shower,
vigorously massage entire body,
avoiding the face and neck area,
and rinse with warm water and feel like new!

Espresso Yourself!
Coffee & Brown Sugar Body Scrub
• • • • • • • • • • • • • • •
Contains: coffee, brown sugar, sweet almond oil,
essential oils of orange and lemon.
To use: open pores in a steaming shower,
vigorously massage entire body,
avoiding the face and neck area,
and rinse with warm water and feel like new!

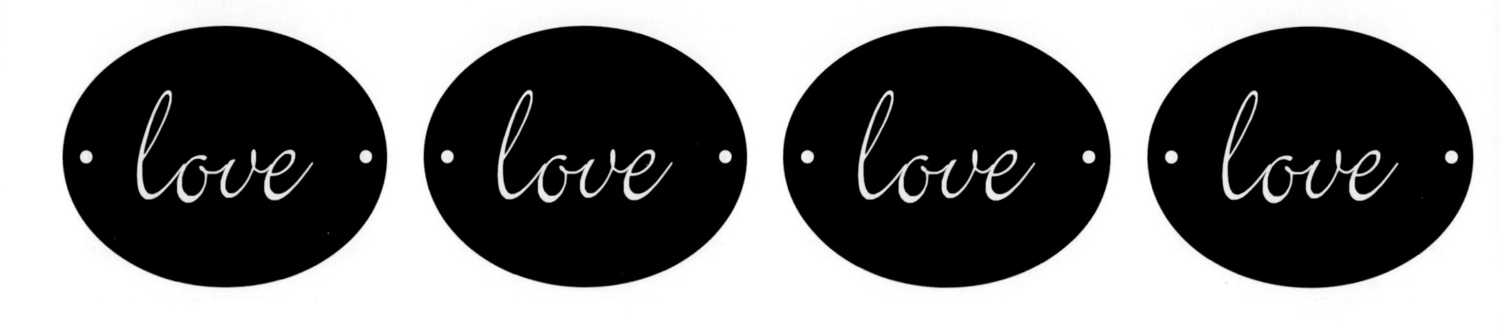

THANKS THANKS THANKS THANKS THANKS THANKS THANKS

A *perfect* DAY

A *perfect* DAY

Rose Water
Glycerin Bath

Rose Water
Glycerin Bath

Rose Water
Glycerin Bath

Rose Water
Glycerin Bath

Rose Water
Glycerin Bath

Cucumber
Kooler

Cucumber
Kooler

Cucumber
Kooler

Cucumber
Kooler

Blow me a Kiss
Cranberry Lip Balm For Sweet Luscious Lips

Blow me a Kiss
Cranberry Lip Balm For Sweet Luscious Lips

Blow me a Kiss
Cranberry Lip Balm For Sweet Luscious Lips

Blow me a Kiss
Cranberry Lip Balm For Sweet Luscious Lips

Blow me a Kiss
Cranberry Lip Balm For Sweet Luscious Lips

Blow me a Kiss
Cranberry Lip Balm For Sweet Luscious Lips

Swing into Spring

Swing into Spring

Swing into Spring

Swing into Spring

Thank you!

Thank you!

Thank you!

Mardi Gras Cajun Spices
Laissez les bon temps roulez – Let the good times roll!

Kung Hey Fat Choy

Mardi Gras Cajun Spices
Laissez les bon temps roulez – Let the good times roll!

Kung Hey Fat Choy

Mardi Gras Cajun Spices
Laissez les bon temps roulez – Let the good times roll!

Kung Hey Fat Choy

Mardi Gras Cajun Spices
Laissez les bon temps roulez – Let the good times roll!

Kung Hey Fat Choy

Bride's Blend

Herbes de Provence

An aromatic mixture, reflecting herbs from the Provence region in southern France.
A combination of thyme, rosemary, sage, basil, summer savory and lavender.
Mix with oil and butter or use as a dry rub on meats, poultry or fish before roasting.
Divine in soups, rice, and pasta. Add a teaspoon to marinades or vinaigrette recipes.
Add a pinch to hot coals for grilling. Bon appetit!

Bride's Blend

Herbes de Provence

An aromatic mixture, reflecting herbs from the Provence region in southern France.
A combination of thyme, rosemary, sage, basil, summer savory and lavender.
Mix with oil and butter or use as a dry rub on meats, poultry or fish before roasting.
Divine in soups, rice, and pasta. Add a teaspoon to marinades or vinaigrette recipes.
Add a pinch to hot coals for grilling. Bon appetit!

Bee
My Honey
***
Deep Conditioner
For Hair

Beach Party BATH FIZZIES

Beach Party BATH FIZZIES

Beach Party BATH FIZZIES

Transferring Patterns

Color-photocopy or trace the pattern onto tracing paper. Use a soft lead pencil to scribble on the back of the tracing paper then place scribbled side down on your decorative paper. Redraw traced lines using a sharp pencil. This will leave light pencil markings on your decorative paper. For a quick transfer method when making multiple favors, use the pattern to draw the outline of the shape onto heavy card stock, then cut out to create a template. Place the template on your decorative paper, then draw around the edges using a sharp pencil. Make a small tick mark at each fold line, then use a bone folder to score the fold lines before cutting out the shape and constructing the box.

Think Outside the Box

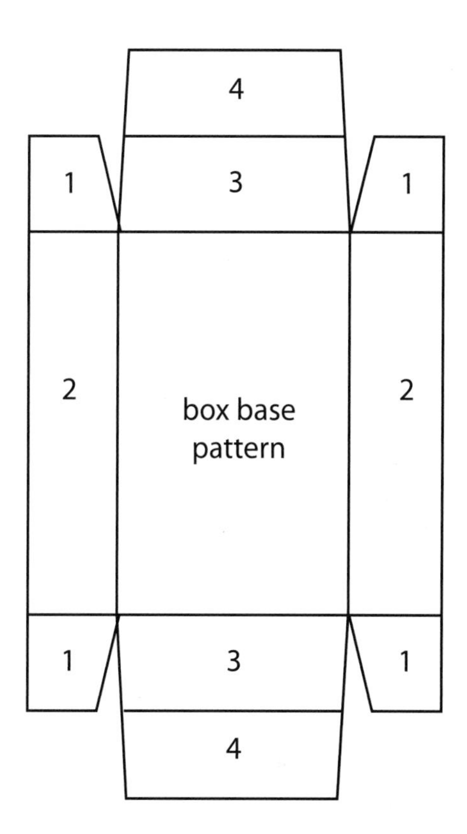

Think Outside the Box

outer sleeve pattern

glue message here

overlap

Purses With Pizzazz

Harlequin Diamonds

purse pattern

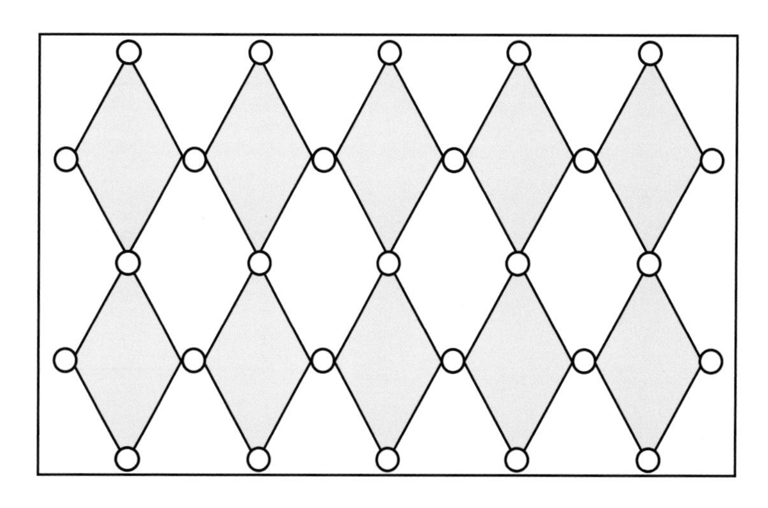

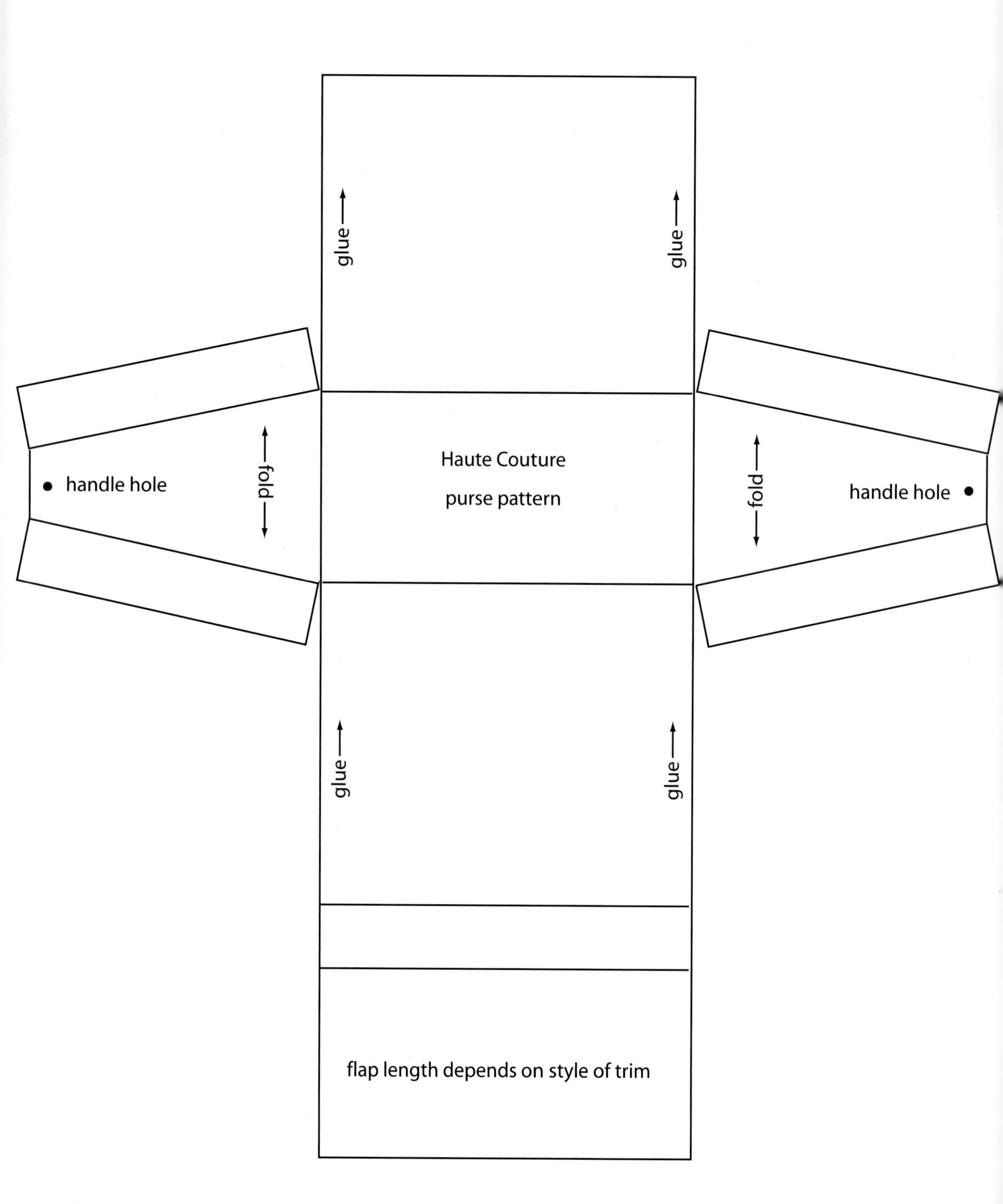
glue
glue
handle hole
fold
Haute Couture
purse pattern
fold
handle hole
glue
glue
flap length depends on style of trim

Swing Into Spring
card pattern

fold

small frame

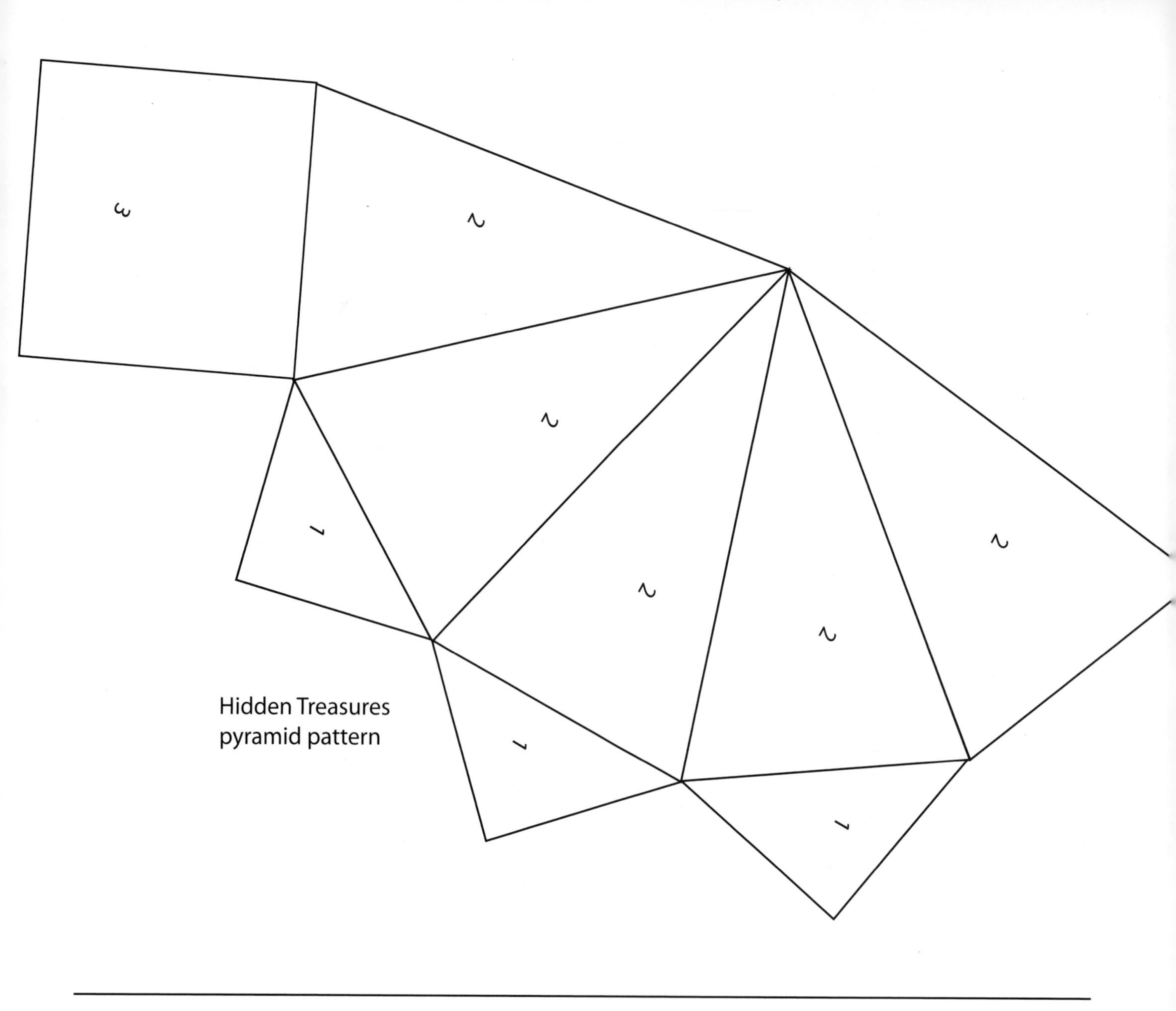

Hidden Treasures
pyramid pattern

Production Team:
- Creative Director: Donna Kooler
- Art Director: Basha Kooler
- Editor-In-Chief: Judy Swager
- Senior Graphic Designer: María Parrish
- Photographer: Dianne Woods
- Photo Stylist: Basha Kooler
- Contributing Artists:
Debby DeBenedetti, Gina Gabriell,
and María Parrish

Produced by:
Kooler Design Studio, Inc.
399 Taylor Blvd., Suite 104
Pleasant Hill, CA 94523
kds@koolerdesign.com

Copyright ©2008 by Leisure Arts, Inc.,
5701 Ranch Drive, Little Rock, AR 72223
www.leisurearts.com

We have made every effort to ensure that these instructions are accurate and complete. We cannot, however, be responsible for human error, typographical mistakes or variation in individual work. This publication is protected under federal copyright laws. Reproduction or distribution of this publication or any other Leisure Arts publication, including publications which are out of print, is prohibited unless specifically authorized. This includes, but is not limited to, any form of reproduction or distribution on or through the internet, including posting, scanning, or e-mail transmission.